ACCELERATED LEARNING

Save Your Time and Increase Your Concentration
for a Lifetime

(A Unique and Revolutionary Guide to Improve
Your Learning Techniques)

Scott Harrison

Published by Bella Frost

Scott Harrison

All Rights Reserved

Accelerated Learning: Save Your Time and Increase Your Concentration for a Lifetime (A Unique and Revolutionary Guide to Improve Your Learning Techniques)

ISBN 978-1-77485-234-7

Legal & Disclaimer

The information contained in this book is not designed to replace or take the place of any form of medicine or professional medical advice. The information in this book has been provided for educational and entertainment purposes only.

The information contained in this book has been compiled from sources deemed reliable, and it is accurate to the best of the Author's knowledge; however, the Author cannot guarantee its accuracy and validity and cannot be held liable for any errors or omissions. Changes are periodically made to this book. You must consult your doctor or get professional medical advice before using any of the suggested remedies, techniques, or information in this book.

Table of Contents

Introduction

We live in a time where things are changing sporadically and if we're not prepared for the changes happening, we'll be in the dust. The best way to be an integral part of the 'life's' strategy is to find ways to be more efficient in learning!

In the present anyone who does not develop quickly loses their knowledge and is unable to comprehend what life is like. They may even say that they are based on their experience. However, that in the world of living your knowledge is as valuable in how effective it can be in helping you tackle difficult issues.

We have established that learning is a requirement and that's true at the very basic stage, and this book is about taking it up to a higher level. To be able to go beyond the basics in your life, you need to think beyond the typical learning rate and consider the growth as well as the retention in the rate of light

The answer is Accelerated Learning!

Accelerated learning is one of the methods of learning and teaching that allows learners to transcend the limitations of their beliefs and assumptions and tap into their untapped potential.

Through accelerated learning, students benefit from a multi-dimensional method of learning. This method allows learners to remember the information they learn in a holistic, natural manner.

If you are thinking about speedy learning, think of an easy way for individuals to acquire knowledge that covers the mental, emotional as well as physically aspects in their life. The student receives a comprehensive learning process that results in an accumulation of efficient and rapid learning methods.

Chapter 1: Enhancing Speed Reading Skills

Reading is the best method of learning. It can also be a factor in rapid learning. Whatever you're looking to learn it must be something to learn about it.

To be able to speed up in the process of learning it is essential to learn to absorb a variety of words and phrases at the same time.

In the first place, reading refers to the process of processing text in order to grasp its meaning. Reading can go beyond just simply looking at words because you need to comprehend the connection between words and their meanings (sense).

Speed-reading is a method used to increase your capacity to read fast. No matter the format of the information required to taken in (digital and physical versions) by speed-reading you will be able to absorb information fast, and that is the primary goal of the program for accelerated learning.

The average person reads 200-400 words per hour, speed readers are said that they read more than 1000 words in a minute.

Reading requires using your ears, eyes mouth and brain, speed-reading requires that you use all these senses, by focusing more on your brain's power.

The brain is a vital component since speed reading demands the most intense concentration. You require focus, full, and constant focus to accomplish this. In order to speed read, you'll have to be able to comprehend and read the language on the page as you think along with the writer.

It is your goal to discern the meaning of what you read in contrast to the normal method of reading. This makes it possible to discern meaning after a time.

This chapter will help to improve your speed reading abilities as it is an essential element of speedy learning. If you wish to master something, you'll need to read, it might not be a novel but it is sure to contain some information.

All the methods you'll find below share one thing that is you must refrain from uttering the word instead, and rather hear the word while reading.

The method that was mentioned earlier was "Sub-vocalization," which is the process of skimming over the words or the group of words you can understand more quickly than you are able to speak the words.

To stop the sub-vocalization it is necessary to focus on the words in blocks instead of individual words. This can be achieved by adjusting your facial muscles and widening your focus towards the page so that you are no longer seeing words as a single entity. The more you work at it, the more your eyes are able to scan more quickly across a page.

Speed reading can be a fascinating experience however, it takes lots of practice using the right methods. This chapter will provide the most effective speed reading strategies in this chapter as well as methods to make the most of these techniques.

Let the speed reading course begin now!

Note that unlike other methods of accelerated learning you've read about The steps listed below have to be done in the same order as that is outlined in this article.

It is only possible to make the most out of the learning process if you adhere to the steps step by step.

1. Go through the Cover Page and Table of Contents

The table of contents is the initial step and it is the first step in laying the foundation for your speed-reading abilities. If you are given a piece of material that you want to study or read, you should first look over the cover and then read the table of contents.

Why is this so important? It's because it communicates with your brain to tell it which parts of the book to check for while reading. Many people believe that speed reading is all about speed learning so that it is possible to skip crucial information however this isn't the case.

It is essential to know the fundamentals to help you comprehend the important subject matter of the text you are reading. This is like the situation when you're about to take a comprehension test and you are instructed to go through the questions prior to reading the text.

The reason behind these guidelines is due to how the brain functions. When you provide your brain with all this prior knowledge, you'll be giving it clues and tips to be aware of as you read.

That is only a sign that you'll read more quickly!

2.Time your reading

After having read this table of contents as well as the the cover page, you must be aware of how long you'd like to take in contrast to the previous reading time. Make sure you read the section that will teach you to determine the speed of your reading later within this section.

However, if you have a certain time frame in your head, it can allow you to establish a goal. This means that you won't spend time distracted. Would you like to be slow to read?

If you assign your brain the responsibility of establishing a timeline, you'll be more dedicated to the reading process. Monitor your progress by keeping track of the time you read.

Try to surpass your previous record since this will inspire you to improve. You can also improve your time by setting a reading target that allows you to set a the number of pages you'd like to read over the time frame and then staying with the goal.

3. Don't use sub-vocalization

This step is vital to speed reading! Subvocalizing is the act of saying words while reading. It is important to avoid reading to yourself as it can cause you to lose focus when you read.

People even chew gum to stop themselves from stumbling over since they realize how crucial it is to end the way they read when they wish to read more quickly.

4.Read the titles and subheadings

In a text materials, you'll discover a variety of headings and subtitles. It is important to read these portions of the book since they offer insight into the contents in the text.

This is similar to studying the table of contents and the front webpage of the text. If you were to read instructions on the best way to prepare spaghetti there would be subheadings like "Ingredients" or "Cooking techniques," skipping these headings will not help you to learn faster since you'll have to determine the contents of the chapter.

If you're in the process of reading an article, begin by reading the title. Keep it in your mind while you read to ensure that you are always aware of the primary idea of the article in the back of your mind when you read.

5. Use a pen , or use your fingers to read

This is by far the most crucial element in speed-reading!

"The Girl had the avocado in a sandwich."

A few people might interpret the above sentence as:

The Girls, The Girl, ate. The girl had an avocado. The girl had an avocado. The girl had the avocado in a sandwich.

What that means is that they are always returning to the first word in the sentence in order to choose the words following it. This type of reading is referred to as visual regression, since the reader isn't making any progress by reading in any way.

The time someone will be spending returning to the beginning "The" as in the instance the speed reader will have moved to further portions of the text.so in order to avoid visual regression, it is essential to employ the most effective speed reading method, which is making use of a pen finger, or a highlighter to read.

When you next read, you should place your fingers on the lines and push them to move while you read at a fast pace. If you do this you'll be able to understand the sentence exactly as it appears:

The girl had an avocado sandwich

Once you've reached "Avocado" as well as "Sand ..." you can proceed to the next paragraph since you are aware there is only one thing you can eat when eating avocado that starts in the form of "Sand" is sandwich.

This is why previous knowledge can also help speed reading.

If your eyes follow your fingers as you scroll through the pages you'll notice that your reading speed improves in time.

This is the most crucial speed reading method as it keeps your eyes from wandering across the page. The focus is on one sentence or a portion or section of the text at the same time.

6.See the word groups

While you are working on avoiding visual regression, make sure you concentrate on a set of words. There are words that you've read before that you are familiar with and when you come across one part in the set, you are able to immediately tell what the next portion will be.

For instance, if you are reading and notice a phrase that reads "The United States of America" it is not necessary to go through the entire sentence because when your eyes first saw "The United States" your brain was already informed that you are familiar with the word.

You finish the task and then move forward. If you can learn to train your brain to scan through different words and phrases, you can save lots of time. It would be difficult to read through many words in the text.

If the text you're reading has diagrams and images it is important to be attentive to them too. Charts or graphs and other representations in pictures are crucial to comprehend and speed reading.

Why do authors use images? The reason is so that the readers will understand the message they're trying to convey through visual format. Through looking at the images, you'll be able to understand the essence of the information without needing to read each word or paragraph.

Check out the footnotes beneath the diagrams, as they can provide a glimpse into the meaning of the diagram and more.

As you look for the words in groups You can also mark crucial words while reading. Be sure to brush your eyes swiftly throughout the entire page in order to grasp what you think is the "Gist" on the webpage.

Take a moment to draw attention to words that contribute to the overall significance on the paper. Begin with words that are repeated and the words repeated many times could be the writer's effort to put the word in the center of attention.

In this portion, the phrase "Speed studying" was repeatedly mentioned. This means that you are able to see it as a collection of words. And wherever you read it, you'll know that the author is highlighting the concept.

Find proper nouns since there are important indicators to look out for to look for underlined and italicized words as well as words you don't recognize. These tips will aid you in getting the most from your reading experience, as you can read faster and more easily.

7. Concentrate on the first and the last sentences

Another method of speed reading is to go through the first sentence of the paragraph as well as the last sentence of the section , instead of simply looking at the middle. The fundamental concept of the book or article you are reading is in the beginning and final sentence.

If you attempt to go through each paragraph with great detail it is likely that you will be lost. For instance, in this particular book in the prior chapter that began you were informed that you'd be learning about "Someone" and the author introduced you by Elon Musk.

If you read the first sentence in the middle, you'll be able to understand the concepts of patterns and how to speed up learning. As you read the very first paragraph, you'll be able to see that it is simple to comprehend the ideas since you've gone through the table of contents previously and know the subject matter.

The reading of these parts of the book can help to avoid reviewing words that you've previously read, as in certain versions, the original text could be a writer's attempt to re-state the main ideas and concepts you've already heard of.

Most books include introductions and summary of every chapter. You should try to concentrate on these. It is also possible to read more quickly once you have a good understanding of the subject.

This method is best when you're reading content that is familiar but you wish to discover fresh ideas.

1. Go faster (yes, you can)

You'll need to be able to move faster than you believe is feasible with speed reading. After you've completed all the above steps, be sure to push yourself to the limit as that's the only way you will be able to truly master this ability.

It is possible to read faster using your hands or pen to read through pages much faster than you typically do or think it is feasible. It's always a surprise when you realize that, speeding up your reading it is also possible to remember and retain the details of the material you're reading. The speed of your reading can dramatically increase as you become aware of the amount of fat you'd like to lose.

The best way to enable speedier reading is to determine the previous reading speed before you began speed reading. This means that right moment you're reading this book, it is important to consider your reading degree of text.

How can you estimate the speed of your reading?

Speed reading is the process of you calculate your speed is known as WORD PER MILLION (WPM) which you can determine it by following the steps listed below.

Take a small portion of a book or other material for 5 minutes , at the speed you would normally read at. Take for granted that you know nothing concerning speed reading up to this time.

Note the place in which you stopped reading.

You should count the number of words that appear in those first 5 lines from the section you have read.

Divide this number by 5 and it will yield the words per the lines (average quantity).

Check the number of pages you have read.

Multiply the number of lines that you comprehend by the words that you are familiar with on strings. (this will yield the amount of words you can read).

Divide the number by 5, and you'll be able to calculate the number of words per minute.

Following the above steps you can determine the speed of your reading and after the calculation, be sure that you create a new reading goal for yourself since now you'll be reading faster.

The best thing about speed reading is that it's a difficult method to master. When you are able to master the art when it comes to speeds reading, it is possible that you will be able to apply the same skills to other areas you are trying to learn.

Remember that the purpose for speed-reading is that you can put into practice what you have read. This means that even if speed read 100 books , if you don't do something making use of the information you've learned from them, your efforts will be wasted.

Do you have a skill you need to master by reading? Try speed reading now and be enthralled by the concept of speeding up using words.

What do you remember about the week before? What did you remember that stuck in your mind?

So, prepare to improve your brain as we discover the importance of photography memory.

Chapter 2: Definitions and Scope

AL is a comprehensive educational program that is rich in contents, yet it's done in the course of a relatively short time.

Acceleratedlearning.info claims that the capacity to retain information is enhanced through AL. Regarding the benefits for learners, the website states: "Their ability to think about systems, critically and creatively grows. They are more proficient and flexible learners!"

From this viewpoint learning is seen as a collaborative process, with the possibility of mutual support. It allows for personal perception and expression. It is humanist, meaning that the transformation of a person's mind is the goal instead of consuming a large amount of information. It focuses on the meaning and significance of information. Furthermore, this method of learning allows exploration, the discovery of knowledge, debate and critique. In other words, AL is a method of learning that is engaged. Instructors promote reflection, inquiry and questioning.

When understood this manner, AL suits the gifted student. It is also suited to those who are more reflective and dedicated or ambitious learner.

According to Acceleratedlearning.info, the following elements comprise the Pillars of AL.

* An Interaction-Rich Learning Environment

In this environment it is possible to have a positive interaction between each student with the facilitators as well as the content and materials used in ways that enhance learning. The physical surroundings encourage interactions, movements, and allows for maximum flexibility in the way it approaches learning.

* Experimentation and Playful Discovery

Learners can have fun playing with concepts and ideas Ask questions, share concepts to the class, examine assumptions and try out different ways to act. The process of discovery creates independent learners and critical thinkers.

* The Arts

The use of collages, music gallery walks, storytelling and improv/theater and other forms of art can make learning an enjoyable and holistic experience.

* State Management

Activities are developed according to the psychological, mental physical, as well as emotional condition of the student to help maintain the best state of mind to learning.

* Suggestions and De-suggestions

Every individual has his own mental beliefs before they embark on an educational program. Participants engage in a variety using a variety of methods to aid in expanding their minds and expand their abilities.

* Reflective Practice

The students are encouraged to think through visual representations of what's occurring, then think about what transpired, and also the actions they took during the period of time. This enhances and helps support the sharing of cognition and learning.

Facilitator Role

Facilitators' roles are crucial because they act as a filter in the learning experience of the student. The AL facilitator should possess these qualities to be successful, including presence in mind, humility, mindfulness and an underlying sense of.

Acceleratedlearning.info has created a map of AL. It shows the course of learning that an AL program by stages that are completed in a specific amount of time.

* The Preparation for the Learner Phase:

The student is prepared physically, mentally and emotionally for learning. The result is a series of exercises that aids in learning throughout the course and even beyond.

The Connection Phase:

The students can discover the significance and meaning of content in their lives.

*The Discovery Phase:

The students are encouraged to participate in the material and learn in different ways. This helps build their skills.

* The Phase of Activation:

Students are encouraged to learn slow and gradually to build their abilities and enable them to use the lessons learned in the future when they return to work.

"The Integration Phase"

Students review their most important learning and formulate new questions and then come up with a plan to go back to their lives.

The proposed learning cycle is in contrast to the more common stages of Western model of education. Some models envision a progression between incompetence and competence. Curriculum is typically linked to a series of lessons (modeling or demonstrating, as well as informing) and students' exercise (written or other types of exercises) as well as review (presenting the same key concepts repeatedly or asking students to explain what they've learned) as well as testing and evaluation using the basis of a rating scale. Most models work from an administrative or institution-or teacher-centered point perspective in which the student receives information, and is required to satisfy the institution's or teacher's expectations.

A model such as the AL scheme proposed by Acceleratedlearning.info intends to be more student-centered. It places students in a positive image, for the first time. Instead of being viewed as being lacking something from the beginning, can be considered to have a contribution to contribute. The student is given a higher position as someone who takes initiative to be involved and making options regarding the interpretation and significance of the subject. The student works with the teacher , and learning is more engaging. It allows more discussion with the teacher, as well as speculation and opinion-forming.

The model presented by Acceleratedlearning.info is an idealist. You may say romantic. But, that's the essence of Western education that is rooted in humanism, and all about personal growth and progress.

In any way, AL has practical purposes and benefits because, no matter the beliefs and hopes of the teachers involved, it's an intensive course that can be which is delivered over a shorter period in time than the class that has weekly classes or modules which are taught over several months. The AL program will require an ongoing, structured and daily studies, which include each day's lessons or tasks that form an integral part of a clearly defined structure of instruction. It's very interactive and students contribute to the learning process by responding to questions, being part of discussions writing and reporting, and being tested on facts and jargon in all directions.

AL provides enriched education. Courses are conducted on strict time frames, which are shortened. Based on time-related considerations this is a good idea. If it's enriched, and by a large amount of educational content however, it is not necessary to compromise quality in the name of efficiency in time.

AL could be a good option for someone who is looking to enhance their qualifications in a short time. It is a great option for those whose education was deferred or not completed, and provides the chance to get caught up. It's beneficial to those companies who, in a rush to meet contract deadlines or reduce costs is looking to have staff trained quickly. A person who wishes to increase or develop themselves for personal reasons might enjoy it. A quick learner will likely appreciate it.

Chapter 3: Learning Transfer

In the words of Elon Musk "persistence is extremely important. It is important to never quit until you are required to give up." Elon Musk's main method of learning is to make sure what he has learned can be put into practice. In order to do this it is essential to understand the ways in which knowledge gained from one field can be transferred to a different field. This is what we refer to as "learning transfer."

Learning transfer involves taking information from a particular field and applying it to another area. The experts on Musk's life see this to be one of the main factors which have led to his success. The process of learning is two-way procedure that is explained in the following paragraphs:

Thinking about things in a different way. If you wish to get greater understanding of a certain thought or idea, it's crucial to examine it from different angles. For instance, let's suppose that you wish to learn more concerning the fraction "1."

Particularly you would like to understand what is the reason why this number is 1. There are two ways that you could approach this topic. One is to consider contrasting situations or differing opinions about the meaning of "1" can mean. However you could consider similar perspectives of the number to get a better understanding. Another option can be helpful when you need to get an understanding of the number or if you apply it to any circumstance, any subject you're learning about. If you're looking to get a more thorough and more comprehensive understanding, then studying various cases is the best option. What can you do to apply this knowledge to your personal life? In any new situation do not just look for "the most effective" method. Don't settle on just one option. Find other options, examine them, contrast and analyze with one another until you discover the basic concepts of the idea that you've received.

"Reconstruct the concepts." Another thing Musk is trying to do is "reconstruct" the concepts which he uncovered during the previous method, but taking into consideration the concepts within the area he wants to apply the idea to. For instance, let's imagine that you have learned about aviation. Then, you can "reconstruct" your thinking about the aviation industry by asking whether the physics involved are comparable to the technology behind more basic things like microwave ovens, and also for business, like online payment processing.

It sounds simple it sounds, but there's much more going into this process than what is possible to described in words. Before you can disassemble and reconstruct knowledge, you must first create the foundation of your own. In the case of Musk it was as follows:

He is a fervent reader. In his early years, Musk would read as many as 60 books in a month.

His interests were differ.

The technique was applied to all things.

The idea behind this is that there's nothing magic or mystical about getting more understanding of what you are learning. Even if you're slow it is still possible to be able to gain speedier learning and apply the knowledge you have acquired to different areas of interest, provided you are able to. It's the matter of which learning procedure you are planning to employ to achieve your goals.

Chapter 4: The Way to Train Your Brain

The brain of the human is an incredible organ. It has proven its capacity to restore memory even when it has suffered an extensive amount of neurologic injuries. Its ability to store information and call specific and pertinent bits of information when required have always been an area of research for many studies. The brain has various parts that are responsible for different aspects in cognitive functioning. The way the parts function and interact in the context of need can result in different levels of learning. The great thing is that your brain is trained to ensure that all its components are working in sync with each to improve learning and memory. That is how the fundamentals of learning speed are set.

Training the brain is possible. It is possible to use different motives for brain training. This is could be the reason you come across with a variety of books with different methods for developing the brain. But, it can't be denied that if this is the situation, there are numerous similarities between these methods. To train the brain to improve recall of memory and better information processing, a collection of the most relevant techniques is summarized.

To make each technique simple to remember, specific names have been assigned to each training technique. They are:

Slow-Cook Method The name says it all slow cooking is an effective method of making someone be more attentive to the particulars. Have you ever made an risotto recipe (like the one on Hell's Kitchen)? If you're not interested in cooking, a regular dose of meditation will work perfectly for you. In the earlier chapter, meditation can improve memory. It's true, it improves memory because it improves the capacity that the brain has to slow down and concentrate on a single focus on one thing at a given time.

Uncomfortable Reading Method: This involves taking yourself out of your comfortable zone and examining things you believe as difficult. The brain, when exposed to challenging tasks or subjects it finds difficult to grasp, is likely to try more. Although the task will require an enormous amount of focus and effort but it's an effective method to develop the brain. The trick is that you should stick to subjects that truly pique your attention. In the absence of this, your project isn't well-defined or has no purpose.

Utilization and Disuse Technique This technique comes from the well-known theory of evolution which is the reason body parts that aren't utilized are removed and those that are regularly used are developed. In the system of accelerated learning the same principle is true for humans' brains. It is important to try to use the parts of your brain that you're not typically likely to utilize. For instance If you're left-handed attempt to use your right hand to prepare for cooking. This will guarantee that both hemispheres in the brain are developed equally.

Learn a New Technique It could be as simple as just a few words per day, a brand new dialect, a dance move, or even the most effective method to get to a particular place. The reasoning behind this is straightforward. The more the brain is utilized and utilised, the better it will perform at the highest level. Maintaining the brain's activity every day will ensure that it's "well-oiled".

Brain-Body Game Method Games that require the body and brain. Yes, puzzles are fun however, they only use an area of the brain that is responsible for reasoning and logic. When you vary the types of games you play, you can have an assurance that all parts of your brain is being utilized. Are playing a ball-catching game beneficial to your brain? It is indeed! This is due to the fact that it requires eye and hand coordination. Additionally, it utilizes the capacity that the brain has to be able to handle information rapidly. The pattern "physical-mental-physical-mental....." in scheduling games to play is an effective way to train the brain.

Question Yourself Method: The practice to do here is about writing the various assumptions you have made about beliefs about a particular thing and then evaluating the credibility of each. You'll be amazed by the types of things you'll find in this kind of brain-training. You'll be talking to yourself, but the benefits are worth it.

The Power in the Music Training Technique Recall the lyrics to a song and then use it to remember details about an area of study that you wish to understand. Music that is familiar to you has been found to be simpler.

The methods described above are not the only methods by which the brain is trained to store, process and remember information. A brain that is properly trained to process these kinds of information can learn at a rapid pace easily. To close this chapter, it is important to be aware that the concepts you have been taught are the core of good habits for studying. If you are looking to improve the habits of study you are aware of then you must move on to the next chapter.

Chapter 5: The Perfect Learning Environment

A conducive learning environment isn't something to ignore since it will allow you to get the most of the opportunity to learn. A learning space is a place where that you feel secure and not distracted It could be your home, classroom or study space. You might be thinking "how do I make a positive learning environment in my classroom? Doesn't it fall to the teachers?" Well, the classroom also has the students in it, and so you can contribute to creating the classroom a more enjoyable learning environment as you are a student. There are nine characteristics that every good learning environment has The first is to be able to ask questions at all times no matter how absurd it might seem. The ability to ask questions is essential to get the most of a learning experience, as it indicates that you are naturally curious and with it an eagerness to study. People tend to avoid asking questions since they don't want to appear uninformed or think the question is too stupid to warrant having an answer. However, it's far than the reality. The most brilliant thinkers are never afraid to ask questions because they realize it's the most effective most effective method to learn. A lot of the greatest thinkers were simply asking questions. Albert Einstein posed the question, "What would the universe appear like in the event that I rode with a beam of light?". This led to the concept of relativity. Isaac Newton posed the question, "Why does an apple fall from the tree?", this lead to the law of gravity. Charles Darwin posed the question, "Why do the Galapagos islands contain numerous species that aren't that are found in other places?", this lead to the theory of evolution.

Value Questions over Answers. As mentioned previously there isn't a issue as a question that is not worthy of consideration and often the question might not be answered immediately. The answer might be a few days, weeks, or a months after the question has been asked. In fact, the question may not provide an answer. The asking a question is beneficial since you're looking into the subject and it's possible that you'll be able to bring up questions that haven't ever been considered before. If that's the case it makes the topic more fascinating. Keep in mind that discovery is

based on questions that are not answered. Consider thinking in a divergent manner. Different thinking can lead to the development of diverse concepts about a subject. To think differently it is necessary to break the subject into manageable, small pieces so that every aspect of the subject can be examined on its own. An approach to come up with ideas from diverse sources is brainstorming which involve creating a list of ideas from diverse source in an unstructured fashion. Any idea that is rejected should be discarded during a brainstorming session, since even though an idea might appear unlikely but it could develop into ideas that seem plausible.

Utilize a variety types of models for learning. Sometimes , you'll need to change your method of learning and this can be accomplished with a range of learning models. For instance, when you're learning about an entirely new programming language it is best not to learn by reading an instructional book, for it is possible that the text will be out of date. It is best to mix to a different approach by doing research online on this language. You can also ask a friend to learn from them, and trying out some programming experiments yourself. Utilizing a array of learning methods will prevent the possibility of becoming bored and keeps the topic interesting and exciting.

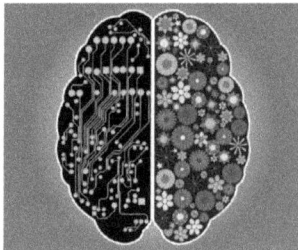

Imagine real-world scenarios. When you're learning, its essential to attempt to link the material you're learning with the real world. Are you reading a novel that is fiction? Make sure you connect the characters to people you know. Good stories have realistic characters that fit into an architype. Sometimes the characters in fiction can linked to real people , and assist you in understanding the characters.

Customize your learning according to the requirements. You should design a learning strategy that is the most appropriate for the content you're learning. If you're studying sports, you'll want to prioritize physical and practice learning over theoretic learning. If you're studying the science of chemistry, for instance, you'll want to do take advantage of as much auditory or visual learning as you can, but add some practical lessons. You can tailor your learning method to the subject you are studying.

Be consistent in your evaluation. Every time you take a learning class consider what have I learned from what level and what I have to master? Recognize when you've struggled with a particular subject, consider the cause of your struggles and what you can do to overcome it for the next session of learning. Check your knowledge regularly. Make a list of the questions that you find difficult, and try to solve these questions. Are you finding the questions too difficult? Continue to practice. Did you find it easy? Find harder questions. Ask for feedback from your the mentor or peers. The information they provide is something to be considered gold.

The aim for success must be apparent. Always set a goal in your mind. If it's to get the best grade in the other students, or to secure your dream job. The way to reach your goal should be clearly defined and you must know the steps to reach it.

Make sure you have ample occasions to work. The most effective tool to learn is practice , and you should ensure that you have every opportunity to exercise. This can be accomplished in many ways. Begin by forming a network of people who are interested in the subject you'd like to master. You'll find that their expertise on this subject is bound to rub over you. How better to master the art of fishing, than by surrounding you with fishermen. It is also important to allow yourself the time to learn. Develop the routine of scheduling your work week to allow you enough time to work out.

Keep your environment tidy. Nobody wants to learn in a messy, unorganized chaos. A clean, tidy environment and organized , you will be able to concentrate on your study. A tidy room leads to the mind being clean.

Combining all of these characteristics is sure to ensure that your learning experience is as flawless as is possible. Keep these things in your head and you'll see your capacity to learn to increase dramatically.

the brain and the brain and

The way your brain learns is highly beneficial in figuring the method you prefer for learning. This chapter will provide information you need to be aware of in relation to learning.

We will first go over the fundamentals that the brain has to offer. The brain has 86 billion nerve cells commonly referred to as neurons. The nerve cell receives signals from other sensory organs, or nerve cells and transmits that information to nerve cells in other areas. The biggest portion of the cerebrum is the brain, that accounts 85 percent of the brain's weight. The cerebrum is split into two hemispheres that are connected through the corpus collosum. It is interesting to note that the left hemisphere is responsible for both sides of your body while the right hemisphere is responsible for that side. The left brain's hemisphere is believed to be responsible for logic-based tasks like writing, reading and speaking, as well as arithmetic comprehension. While the right part of brains is thought to be more creative that require visual perception and music, pattern recognition and emotion.

It is said that individuals are either right or left brain dominant, the same way that they could be left or left hand dominant. Someone with a brain that's "left brained" is thought to be more rational and analytical, as well as objective. Someone that is "right brained" is thought to be more reflective and intuitive. They are also more subjective. It turns out that the concept of left and right dominance of the brain is an old psychological mythology that developed out of observations about the brain which were severely distorted. However, it's interesting to note that this myth remains accepted despite having been disproved. However, knowing what your weaknesses and strengths are will assist you in developing more effective ways to learn. For example, if have difficulty listening to lectures, it could be beneficial to note down the content of the lecture as well as re-reading your notes.

How does the brain develop? To answer this question, one should be aware of the concept of plasticity, or to be more precise that is, neuroplasticity. Neuroplasticity is the brain's ability to grow and change throughout your life. When you are learning anything new in your life, the brain adapts physically through strengthening its neural connections, aswell in creating new connections. Imagine learning how you can play guitar the very first time. Your brain is in the middle of figuring it all to the brim. It needs to manage all of your senses: what you experience as well as hear and see. You'll be thinking about everything that you have to think about in order to play the guitar. Your motor skills will be put on the test while stringing the guitar. You'll be listening to the music you play, and how the sound is synchronized with the movements of your body. Your brain is storing precise timings as well as co-ordinating the actions you require. Your brain is developing new neural connections to improve the memory of movements in the music. These things happen at the same time in your brain without you even noticing it. When you first take the guitar out it is likely that you will make a few mistakes. However, with time and practice your brain will grow and strengthen neural connections dedicated to playing guitar. The more you practice, the more strong the neural connection grows until you are able to learn how to play the guitar. Learning gets completed.

There are a few things you need to know about the brain in order to get the most of your lessons that can speed up the strengthening of your brain. Humans are visual beings and, of all our senses, we depend on our vision the most. Therefore, it is natural that we are the best at processing visual information. The reason is that the brain contains a large number of neurons dedicated to processing visual information. About 30 percent of neurons that make up the cortex focus to processing information from visual sources. This is a significant portion of your brain dedicated to processing information of your eyes. Humans are also extremely sensitive to movement. We've evolved this way to prevent being snatched by predators. We don't have to be concerned about being snatched away by ambush predators, however, we have a keen sense of the movement. Therefore, it should come as not a surprise that video and visualisations are an excellent way to improve your knowledge.

We are prone to forgetting small aspects. While learning something for the first time it's easy to get focused on the small details and end up overwhelmed. One way to prevent this is to consider the bigger overall picture. When you're learning something new it is possible that your brain will lose things if it is unable to identify prior knowledge that is relevant. If you take a look at the whole image it provides your brain with something it can go back to and connect to while processing the new information. A metaphor can assist you in visualizing this concept. Imagine your brain as the shelves in a closet, as you accumulate more clothes, they take up more space on the shelves and you begin to categorize them. If you add any new information, for example, an oversized black sweater, it could be placed on the winter shelf, the black shelf or the sweater shelf. In real life , you are unable to put your clothes in more than one place however in your mind, the new piece of information becomes connected to concepts that are already in place and makes it easier to recall the new piece of information.

Sleeping patterns affect your ability to learn. Research has shown that having an adequate night's rest between learning sessions can improve your brain's capacity to keep information. In a research study that focused on motor skills, it was observed that those who had the best night's sleep for within 12 hours of having learned something new increased their skills by 20. Participants who were tested at four hour intervals throughout the daytime were only able to improve their skills by four percent. When you're studying or taking exams, ensure you're and rested. Are you having trouble getting enough sleeping? Consider taking naps throughout the daytime. Research has shown that taking naps provide the same advantages as an uninterrupted night's sleep. A nap prior to a class has also been proven to have great benefits. It was said by Dr. Matthew Walker, a principal researcher from the University of California has said "Sleep helps the brain become a sponge that's dry, prepared to absorb fresh information". If there's one factor that you'd like to avoid while learning something new is sleeping in a slumber. Research has shown that lack of sleep is a major negative factor on learning new skills as it reduces the ability to learn that the brain has by as high as 40. When you are learning the new skill ensure that you have a good night's sleep and if you don't take it, take advantage of it by taking napping. This will help you maximize the learning experience.

The brain learns the best when you teach others. When you're teaching other people it's natural to organize information in a different way in your brain, and remembering information becomes much easier. In one study by Dr. John Nestojko, half of the participants were told that they'd be tested on a topic they were studying. Another half were told they needed to impart to others what they've learned. The two groups needed to pass tests, but they didn't need to impart their knowledge to anyone. Incredibly, it was observed that those who were told that they needed to impart knowledge to someone received higher than those who were told they were being assessed. This suggests that the mind of the learners prior to learning has a huge impact on the learner's abilities to learn. When you're learning, you can fool yourself into thinking that you're likely to be teaching to others or even instruct other people. This way, not only will you be benefiting yourself by enhancing your ability to learn as well as benefitting others by teaching them.

Chapter 6: Worst Way To Learn

Before we go through the steps to focus on learning, practicing and eventually mastering our skills it is important to consider a completely different environment far from the idyllic spaces that we imagined in Chapter 1. A environment that's more challenging to learn in. This is the case with school. One of the reasons to address this issue is because school, for a lot of individuals, has lots of mental baggage. The students develop negative opinions about learning and their ability to learn from a variety of unintentional influences that happen in the classroom. Let's get rid of that baggage.

There is a Problem with School

For many, schools are not the ideal learning environment in which we are required to remember a myriad of facts without being provided with an understanding of the framework or an explanation for why we should care. We're taught to recite lists that we're not interested in and we know we'll never need. Although the most skilled teachers might attempt to make traditional education enjoyable, there are fundamental issues with the way that public schools are designed that hinders motivation and may cause negative attitudes towards learning. I'll provide these issues below.

Learning through Rote

While educational theorists advocate more active learning for classrooms, in reality most of the job of a typical student is to memorize and repeat facts. This is referred to as rote learning.

The issue with rote learning is that there's often very little context to the knowledge you're looking to learn. One illustration can be The periodic table. A lot of Middle school teachers request their students to remember their periodic tables. The table is an instrument for scientists who work in a variety of disciplines, memorizing what the proper names are for all the elements in the table is simple memorization if you don't have the sufficient background knowledge.

The names that appear on the table of periodic elements were chosen over the course of centuries by scientists across the globe. It is, with no additional context, just a sequence of sillables. Understanding the names will get nothing closer to understanding the way electrons are shared between atoms in a covalent bond. it simply illustrates that you can keep a list of them in your mind. When the goal is making a list, the absence in context can make it difficult to complete. It's difficult to understand this set of names as there's no information to grasp that isn't helpful to you in your everyday life and has no value in comprehending the science.

The issue with rote learning is that the absence connectedness to the meaning of what we learn makes it hard for us to come up with a solution using the information we've taken into. We aren't able to apply it to an entirely different situation because we aren't able to comprehend its context. Application of knowledge outside of the context in which it was originally learned by taking what you've learned then applying that knowledge to a different context, is referred to as generalization, and is regarded by academic theorists as an increase in understanding. Learning through repetition won't bring you to the top.

The underlying message behind the practice of memorization by rote can be that it is to be remembered, but not understood. This is how we are taught in schools and is completely contrary to the way we should take our learning. Remember the state capitals. Remember how to multiply tables. Memorize important dates in history. However, don't fret about the meaning that go behind these lists, or the reason we use these lists in the way we do. For many, learning by rote is a painful and unpleasant mental work. We'll discuss this in Chapter 3. for some , memorizing is effortless, while for others it's very difficult.

I've always been a terrible memory-maker. My brain tends to place things in wider contexts, and making connections between different things. I find that I remember things better after I have a grasp of the larger picture, but my view of remembering to gain understanding does not make sense. I am mentioning this as an example of how that schools can lead to negative attitudes. By promoting this kind of non-contextual learning, they increase the stress of students (at the very least, those with brains not built to remember) which could lead to an attitude of disinterest towards learning, or even a negative image of oneself.

It's also important to remember the fact that learning with no understanding can be incredibly boring. Children are more likely to react negatively to boring tasks. Do we really want to teach them they are boring when learning?

Arbitrariness

In today's classrooms teachers work on a list of "standards of learning" which dictate what needs to be taught and how to teach it. They are put together through a series of choices made by a panel composed of "experts" which includes administrators, teachers officials, bureaucrats, as well as politicians. They decided the selection of rules is the best for the students as well as the teachers who must adhere to the guidelines. When something is drafted by committee members, it's not a comprehensive document. It's a compromise exercise.

Different experts have their own plans; they disagree over compromises, then adjust until you are left with a strategy that is best to meet all these competing needs at the same time. It is often an unsatisfactory plan where the components do not connect and one that makes it difficult for students to comprehend the reasoning for the reasons behind the choices about the direction of their studies. In reality, adhering to the government-mandated set of guidelines can appear to be an unconnected series of lessons.

What message does this convey to students? Educational philosophers discuss how important it is to develop lifelong learners. This is something I'll cover at the end of the book and it's an important one. Teachers must view this as an essential part of their responsibility to instill the love of learning in their students, as well as an equal desire to keep developing and improving themselves by acquiring it over time. It sounds great, doesn't it? But it's only a theory.

Teachers have to prepare to pass the test which is something that students know about. They know they'll have subjects to test in the near future. They are usually told precisely what subjects will be covered. It's a message that is not positive that is very practical. The field of knowledge isn't endless to explore over an entire life. It's a collection of boxes to be crossed off. Did you master the set of sixth grade standards? Excellent. The time is now to begin the curriculum for seventh grade. The curriculum makes education as dull as is possible, and also contributes to a shallow approach to the subject.

Relevance

The majority of what we learn in school isn't relevant to our daily lives. Teachers who are the best strive to change this. For instance for instance, the American Revolution can be an unintentional series of dates, names and battles. However, when it is taught by an excellent teacher, it could be brought to life. Students will find something they can identify with in the characters of the founders. The self-determination motive that sparked the revolution could be made more appealing to an impulsive teenager. Making these connections, topic-by-topic throughout the entire school year requires lots of effort along with time, which teachers usually do not have. Particularly when we're young it's easy to glance at a boring history textbook and think that it's no relevance to your life.

In terms of development, children generally tend to focus on themselves. This is logical, right? When a kid is fortunate enough to have an environment that is conducive to parenting They are taught from birth that they're in a sense the most important thing in the world. Parents go to great lengths to ensure they're well-nourished and healthy as well as safe. Even when they're being punished, they have this feeling that everything is focused on them. While toddlers are able to tell the signs that other people are unhappy their emotional state is a bit tangled.

In adolescence, egocentrism increases. Research has found that adolescents underestimate their importance or their uniqueness. Sometimes, they even have the mental image of an imaginary audience an unknown crowd of fans cheering them on similar to the studio audience that's invisible beyond the fourth wall, to the left of an unnoticed camera.

While it might sound like a fantasy but this is a common development and something we can get over. However, asking children to study facts without demonstrating how it is related to his own life, could create a bad taste in his mouth and put a worry about his future education.

Practical

This follows naturally from the arrangement of the previous one. If you're young who believes all the world revolves around your, then you're always asking "Why should I bother?" If what you're required to learn has any relevance to your present life and has no relevance for your future So why be concerned? It's difficult to make schoolwork meaningful, and it could be difficult to prove that it's useful. A teacher could argue that studying and passing each standard in all subjects is crucial to the future of a student because they must complete their studies in order to graduate and also to be able to be able to apply to colleges with high scores.

It's similar arguments about college. These courses are essential to allow you to pursue the subjects you're interested in or which provide you with the job and life you'd like to live. Perhaps in these classes, you'll need to make a few alterations depending on the needs of the instructor however, these are also required if you're hoping to succeed. This argument rarely is a convincing argument. You need to pass because you must pass in order to pass. It's basically sayingthat you must jump through hoops to get the information you want to know.

I'm not saying there's no reason to have an excellent Liberal Arts foundation. I am a believer in it and believe it's a solid foundation to create an understanding between educated individuals. However, I think that by not making the case for why certain information is essential schools can in creating a negative mindset toward education, which could result in failure and follow students for the rest of their life.

A lot of students develop an unfavourable attitude toward education from an early age. This can lead to a tragedy. Reading is a great illustration. Similar to what I've said about memory. The brains of different people function in different ways. For certain people readers, reading is the most simple technique to learn anywhere in the world. They can learn it by themselves. Our son is born with a language-related brain and he began to learn at the age of three. When he entered kindergarten, he was able to read at the fourth grade level. It's a great feeling to be proud of an adult but really it's the chance that happens. They can be described as considered to be the Jimi Hendrixes in the field of literacy. They possess the natural talent that can be developed.

For some, it's difficult. The problem isn't that the kids aren't smart, but their brains aren't the same in the area of reading. They may need additional assistance and guidance to master reading. If kids don't receive this assistance, they may feel that reading isn't worth it. If they see Jimi Hendrixes in the class quickly "getting that," they feel dumb. They feel like they're failing. They stop trying. It's not long before the potential for reading diminishes and literacy becomes an ever-growing and bigger hill to conquer. It's not only a matter of cognitive ability, but also mental attitude and psychological.

If you're unable to read, you'll be unsuccessful in a lot of subjects. You could certainly be able to master math, but you'll need to be concerned about problems with reading. Failure to get over the initial hurdle and master to read has lead to a negative outlook toward education, which is an unfulfilling prophecy about academic failing. They are often disruptive in the classroom because they don't know the situation and do not feel that they are rewarded for trying. What's the answer "what's to gain from this?" Nothing. Failure to cultivate an attitude of gratitude towards education can, in a few instances, end up destroying young people's lives. To be clear, I'm not saying that teachers are responsible for this. They are often doing their best work as they are able to. The issues with education are systemic , and are not easy to fix. A lot of people with good intentions are working to improve their education, but the deck appears to be against the progress.

Do you wish to hear positive news? The information I've provided is not the way we'll learn. Be aware that the course you studying will be guided by you. You will get exactly what you want to know in a specific and systematic manner.

The significance of Extrinsic Motivation

When it is properly executed, is a far superior option than being subject to the vagaries and whims of an education system that has numerous moving pieces as well as poor top-down communication. Self-motivated learning solves two of three identified issues. If you choose to learn somethingnew, it's a personal choice. Whatever the reason for which you've decided to study a new subject or master an area of expertise and the freedom to choose is what makes it meaningful for you personally. It doesn't matter if you're learning HTML programming to advance your career, or picking up the ukulele to entertain guests at events, the fact that this is the kind of training you've completed by yourself is a sign of something. This means that your goals are dependent on your own will.

Through the majority of our formal educational experiences our motivation is intrinsic. Extrinsic motivation comes from what is forced upon us by the outside. As kids we attend school because we're expected to. Our parents forced us to. We didn't have a choice. If you're struggling with your grades Perhaps your parents attempt to convince you to do better by inflicting a penalty or giving you an incentive. In each of these situations no matter if we're talking about sticks or carrots it's an extrinsic motivation and is imposed by someone else.

In college, we're required to follow a strict planned course of studies, with many insignificant aspects in relation to our objectives. It is possible to want to be at the top of our game in the most broad sense however, a lot of what we learn in college is imposed on us. For instance, if are certain that you would like to be an engineer of chemical origin You still must complete the same set of electives in general education as students of other schools. You may also need to complete the major prerequisites in order to take the classes you are interested in (assuming that your passion for chemical engineering doesn't come instilled by an external source). You must go through these hoops to be able to access the classes that you're interested in. Classes that you are interested in serve as a reward that makes you want to complete the necessary prerequisites. The core classes are intrinsically stimulating and create an extrinsic incentive to leap through the hurdles.

Internal motivation originates from the self. It's when we discover something that is intrinsically compelling. Behaviorists collaborate with children, especially children with autism to modify their behavior through the use of rewards and after which they gradually reduce the rewards to induce the behavior. Chemical engineering fundamental courses that we discussed earlier are intrinsically motivating when the motivation to become a chemical engineer is genuine and personal.

If you decide to educate yourself, you are in essence, showing an intrinsic drive. If you're looking to master Mediterranean cooking then you are able to move on to acquiring relevant information and acquiring the necessary abilities. There is no authority outside of your home to require you to complete an trigonometry class before you get to the best part. If you study on your own you can choose what you'll learn, and without any unnecessary filler or fluff, thus keeping your motivation constant throughout the course. The process of organizing your own learning liberates you from the burdens of traditional schooling and lets you focus only on the things you'd like to master. We'll go over organizing your educational plan in chapter 4.

I'll repeat the point that I'm not seeking to discredit the concept or the value of a traditional Liberal Arts education. It is valuable and if your objective is to attain the exact result, a university can be beneficial. But we're talking about in this article. It's about how to gather the knowledge or expertise you want and executing it in a targeted and quick manner. Knowing how best to accomplish this requires review of the science behind retention and memory , and how we can implement it.

Chapter 7: Tips For Learning And Recollecting Information

Mnemonics are a technique for learning which is employed to enhance the retention of key information. The aim of this method is to connect items that are already memorized to new information using acoustic or visual signals. In essence, we look for the common sound or image to link something similar to the new thing we wish to remember.

The advantage of having a mnemonic system is that it is able to be modified by every person in order to make it easier for them to learn. It is a simpler method to increase memory. Mnemonics can help you retain information that is essential to understand.

Make and begin using the Strategy Today

Use mnemonics to help you remember crucial information. When you're in college, it's essential to do everything you can to ease your life since you face many pressures every day. This is also true for entrepreneurs. This strategy is applicable to everyone. The best part is that the mnemonics are easy to master by yourself.

Keywords

Keywords are the words that are easily understood by the idea being recalled or learned. Instructors typically explain their ideas by connecting the new information with something they are aware that students have already stored in their minds. For instance, ranidae is a kind of frog. If instructors were to impart this knowledge, they could show their students an image of frogs jumping in the rain. This would associate "rain and Frogs" to "ranidae," making it stay in memory.

Pegwords

Pegwords are a well-known form of mnemonics that are employed in our modern day society. This strategy of learning makes use of rhymed words to help memorize numbers. For instance, the word to describe "one" will be "bun." The pegwords for 1-10 are:

*One = Bun

Two = Shoe

*Three = Tree

*Four = Door
*Five = Hive
*Six = Sticks
*Seven = Heaven
*Eight = Gate
*Nine = Vine
*Ten = Hen

The list is easy to recall. Once you've memorized the list, you can make use of it to study facts in a particular order. For instance, if you must remember that spiders have eight legs, then draw a quick sketch of a spider perched on an entrance.

Acronyms

Then, we get to acronyms. This is another kind of mnemonics that's extremely useful. Acronyms (also known as first letter Mnemonics) utilize the first letter in each word to create a distinctive word that is easier to remember. Actually, it's possibly the most effective method of memorization using mnemonics that are available to you. I am sure you have several of these written down which you may not be aware of.

Two excellent instances of the First Letter Mnemonics that are taught to students in the school curriculum are HOMES and PEDMAS.

It is the abbreviation HOMES uses to explain the names used by the Great Lakes:

Huron

Ontario

Michigan

Erie

Superior

The PEDMAS program is designed to help students learn how to teach the Order of Operations in math:

Brackets and Parenthesis

Exponents

Division

Multiplication

Addition

Subtraction

This method to remember any kind of information. We see it in ads and in business often. The idea is simple that it's simpler to memorize one word than it is to learn multiple words.

Paired Associates Strategy

Paired association is a method to acquire information in pairs. Examples of this kind of information include names, dates, events, and locations or even accomplishments and locations. The paired association strategy has been demonstrated to significantly increase the retention rate of associated information. In essence, you will need do these things to employ the paired association strategy

*Identify details

Create an memory device

Note it down.

*Learn about the details

Now that you've figured out the purpose of the strategy, let's take more in depth review of the process required.

We adhere to the CRAM process here.

Make a mental image.

Connect to something else.

Arrange

Create a code.

Example

Typically, Paired Association is used after all alternatives are exhausted, and the majority of students use this strategy for dates because it's difficult to connect pictures to dates. In this regard, let's examine an example of this technique using it in the real world.

Abraham Lincoln was assassinated in 1865. Create a mental image: It is impossible to connect an image in our minds with the date.

Connect to another event It is possible to relate this to the day that Andrew Johnson was President. You can only do this when you had to recall the dates of Andrew Johnson's time during his presidency.

Organise: If we are able to keep in mind both the day on which Abraham Lincoln was assassinated and the year that Andrew Johnson was president, then we can combine this data with this information.

Create an Code: Pairing a date begins by creating an alphabetic number. In this case, we'll use the formula 1=A, 2=B and 3=C and so on. We will change 1865 to the letter format that reads: A, H, F, and E. Then, use these letters to create an expression that is related to the data. I'll use a non-politically accurate example:

Abe's Head was Found to have exploded.

All we need to do is to convert this unforgettable phrase back into the format of a number.

Abe's = 1

Head = 8

Found = 6

Exploded = 5

It's not a great image, but it's very memorable. Be careful not to say the words aloud!

The strategy may appear complicated, but it's not. In reality, it's more difficult to explain than to apply.

LINCS Vocabulary Strategy

The second tip is to master new vocabulary terms applying a proven method called the LINCS Vocabulary Strategy. If you are struggling to master new vocabulary or are seeking a method to reduce the time you spend studying This is the ideal approach for you! Are you eager to start?

First thing to remember to remember is LINCS can be a shorthand that helps you remember the steps.

Check the Parts

Find the Word that Reminds You

Note an LINCing Image

Make a LINCing Picture

Self-Test

In that regard below are the main methods required to use this strategy. LINCS Vocabulary Strategy.

Preparation

Find words you struggle with and write down any facts that you need to be able to recall by using those words. It is possible to start with the complete definition however most students find it simpler to simply write down the most important aspects. In any case, you'll need have to break it down in just a few minutes.

Get the index cards out and get ready to begin writing!

Here's the word we'll use to show these steps:

Word: Palisades

Definition A steep line of high cliffs along the shores of an ocean or river.

Step 1 Step 1: Make a list of the parts

Write down the word you're trying to remember on the index card's front. Turn the card over and write the essential summary in the form of a definition, on the reverse side of your index card. You can then circle the word you're learning to give it the emphasis.

Utilizing Our Example

The front of the card: Palisades

Back of card A line of steep high cliffs that runs along the ocean or river.

Step 2: Choose an Reminding Word

Find words that have an identical sound to the word you're trying to master. It's crucial that the word does not just be similar in sound however, it also will remind you of its definition. The word you are reminded of should be written on the reverse of the index card, which contains the word.

Effective reminder words should always include any one of these:

*Sounds like an English word (or at the very least a portion of it).

Be something you've already discovered. It's not good to connect a word with something isn't yet learned.

Be sure to test it to see if it is a reference to what you're trying master.

Your attention should be directed towards the definition that you have to keep in mind.

Utilizing Our Example

Remembering Pal

Step 3 : Record an LING Story

In this moment, I realize that this concept is like a lot of confusion, but it will become clear in a minute. Make your own LINCing story by connecting your word that you are reciting and the meaning of the word you're trying to remember. Put this on the index card.

Utilizing Our Example

My LINCing story: My friend, Bob, loves to plunge off the cliffs to the sea.

Note: The sentence in our example is very simple, but employs"cliff," i.e "cliff" to refer to the meaning of our primary word. That's how we connect "pal" to "cliff."

Step 4: Design an LINCing image

On the reverse of the index card, sketch an image depicting the story you created. This will help you visualise the LINCing word.

Step 5: Test Yourself

After you've created the index cards for every word you have to remember Make a mix of them and then go through them to test your knowledge.

"Speak the new word loudly.

Say the word that reminds you aloud.

Recite your LINCing story loudly.

Take a close look at your LINCing photo.

* Without taking a look at the reverse of the card read what the meaning of this word in a loud voice.

Check the reverse side of your card and determine whether you are correct.

*Repeat each word over and over until you've memorized every word.

Making Notes and Listening

It's true that you'll spend a significant amount of time in lecture halls, and learning to maximize the knowledge you acquire in this time will allow you to free up lots of time outside of the classroom. I believe that the classes are the most important time of the day because that's the time when students tend to fall off the track. Unfocused in class leads to the necessity to study for exams , which increases the time you spend studying.

If you follow these three simple steps, you'll be able to save your time. You must be present in the classroom, and you must get the most out of it.

1. Adopt excellent listening skills.

2. Note down your notes clearly and concisely. (Record the lecture, if permitted.)

3. Make sure to review your notes within 24 hours after taking them.

Let's take a look at each step in greater in detail.

Adopting Effective Listening Skills

First, you need making it to class before the time to ensure that you have the best seat free of distractions. I strongly suggest to place yourself near your front room as you can. While you wait for class to start, go over your notes from prior lectures. This will let you think about the topic and ideas that could be discussed.

When the lecture starts Write down any major ideas and pertinent details to support these concepts. Pay attention to when your instructor begins to review the information you've learned. They do this via talks or by spending lots of time on one particular concept.

Listening effectively is a 2-way process and you should often ask questions when are unsure about the meaning of something.

Writing concise, clear notes

Notes that are taken well are an important step. I'll walk you through a precise procedure that has been proved to be effective.

1. Only draw on only one paper. Draw a line vertically , about 1 inch away from the left side on the page. Then draw a horizontal line just a few inches away off the top of your page.

2. Note down your notes on the center of the page. It is not necessary to write down

every word the instructor speaks. Concentrate on the key concepts and ideas. Make note of only the important details such as illustrations or examples instructors provide. If, for instance, the instructor gives you an PowerPoint presentation, then you should record every single thing on the slide.

3. Make sure that you are consistent with the abbreviations you use. Be sure you can easily can comprehend the meaning of each.

4. Make sure to mark the transition from one idea to the next by skipping over a line.

5. If you don't remember an idea or a date and you aren't sure, make a space in which it is possible to add it later.

6. Utilize the margin on your left (left from your vertical line) to note notes that require more research.

Examining your Notes

Review your notes every 24 hours. The reason for this is that your brain transforms information stored in short-term memory into long-term memory while you sleep. This means that you have to go over information when it's stored in the short-term memory. This is the reason why students lose most of the information they've learned in less than 24 hours. Take advantage of this review time to:

* Fill in any blank areas on your notebooks.

*Respond to questions from the lecture.

Make use of the area just to your left the vertical line to write down important concepts, dates, and other pertinent details. This can be helpful when studying to take an exam.

Use the space below the horizontal line to write down a overview of your page. When you've got more than one webpage of the same subject or subject and you want to summarize it, you should do so each page every two to three pages.

This is because the information is being linked even while it's still within your memory of the moment. This makes it better after it's been transferred to your long-term memory.

Chapter 8: Outlook And General Learning Approach

Develop an attitude of encouragement for the continuous advancement of your career.

Before you can take on the responsibility to pursue a subject first, you must determine what kind of person you are. It is essential to develop and promote a spirited flexible, free-thinking, and moldable mentality. There are two primary kinds of learners that people are inclined to classify themselves as. The first is being naturally intelligent, born with all the knowledge and unwavering characteristics. The other is being an ever-in-progress learnerwith no fixed levels of intelligence built in learning, and knowledge increasing or decreasing based on how they perform their tasks and carry out their job. This is the more proper way of looking at oneself. A man known as Josh Waitzkin, a chess master and martial arts champion and expert in speed-learning, describes the two mental models as "entity" as well as "incremental." To be able to get the most value out of your ability to learn over the course of your entire life you should follow the incremental method of thinking. In this is the way to go, no matter if you succeed in completing tasks or not, you'll realize that the final result depends on your efforts. This is based on the amount of effort you place into these activities in addition to the effectiveness of your method or learning strategies. If you take your learning seriously and put in the appropriate amounts of energy, you'll be able to grasp concepts and increase your knowledge in any area, gradually but steadily until you're proficient in it. Unfortunately, the majority people adhere to the concept of an entity. In this manner they believe they have no say in how well they perform tasks or not, since their ability is inherent to their capabilities and they don't have the option to change it. In this way, it's almost impossible to conquer the inevitable obstacles and difficulties encountered when learning new information. When faced with challenges They tend to break easily, and often become angry and depressed to the point that they are ready to give up. People believe they are supposed to be static and stagnant They are scared of making a change.

The first thing to do to effectively acquire new information and develop new skills is to separate your personal identity from the information you're acquiring. You must realize that in the process of learning it is essential to get out of your box. Recognize that you'll be exposed, and decide to continue pushing forward regardless whatever obstacles you are confronted with. Take a look back at any instances in your life that you gained knowledge and how you responded to the challenges you encountered along the journey. Did you lose when difficulties came up or did you persist to overcome them? Set a goal to grow into an enlightened incremental thinker and acknowledge your potential as a moldable and awe-inspiring person you are. Learn to accept any challenges you encounter and utilize them as part of the process of learning. To accomplish this, it is important to remain humbleand admit that there are things you aren't aware of. There are a lot of things you're initially unable to do and you'll confront these issues in the process of learning.

The most famous basketball player of all time, Michael Jordan, strongly believed in this idea. While he showed abilities that made him superior than his peers but he was still willing to listen to his teammates and coaches. Even if he had doubts regarding their suggestions or concepts but he was willing to try to give them a chance. This is that he was aware that the possibility existed that his beliefs were not true which is a great example of humility. To be able to master a subject efficiently and quickly it is an essential quality you have to develop to yourself. The incremental approach may be difficult to comprehend however, it's not at all impossible. If at any point in your journey to learning, you begin to feel demotivated, go to the chapter (as as well as any later ones) to be able to get back into the correct mental attitude. The struggle and the discomfort are positive, and signify that you've been taking the correct path. If you're capable of absorbing information faster than other people, as you'll be after having read this book, everything you learn will require some time and energy. If you are embarking on a quest to learn something new or gain an ability that is new it is important to recognize that it won't take place in a single day, and to take every stage of the learning process. The next chapter will help you to increase your tolerance for stress and, more specifically, how to turn the negative feelings and transform them into positive experiences.

Learn to deal effectively with Disappointments and Errors

It is essential to stay positive throughout the whole process of learning. Keep your mind focused and calm, just like the way a child behaves when they learn something they love. They aren't paying attention to the surrounding world or any other concerns; they're absorbed in their activities and enjoying the process. They are completely focused on the task at hand and exploring, and they don't have any concerns about the possibility of failing. The best chance to avoid being discouraged and departing from their relaxed attitude is if you fail to master to master a new skill. As a result, it is essential to know how to deal with any mistakes that you make when doing your best effort. If you do make a mistake you'll need to get back into an open, calm and focused mental state as quickly as is possible. For a metaphor, imagine of your joyous learning as a vessel with a smooth and easy sailing across the ocean. The breeze fills the sails and the journey ahead is thrilling and optimistic about achieving your goal. If the sun is shining with a gentle breeze blowing through you are confident and inspired while learning. However, adverse weather can be expected when you travel for a long time.

Unexpected dark clouds may appear as well as heavy rains and wind that throw you off your course. If this happens you are worried about whether you will be able to reach your goal and get to the location you have indicated in your plan. The ship is swinging one side to the other, and you are feeling uneasy. What you must do is to regain your balance and get in the direction you had been. Return to your path in the shortest time possible and then resume the easy, smooth journey you had originally been taking.

Don't let the rough seas force you to quit and end your journey. Be aware that weather storms are normal and it is best to learn to deal with it and stay through the point of no return. Don't give up and let it slam your boat. Be aware that even if clouds block your view but the sun is visible behind them. This is especially difficult to keep in mind if you find yourself making the same mistake several times over and over. If you make this mistake, it's easy to get frustrated and angry and feel like throwing out the window. It's easy to conclude that you're ineffective of this ability, and you're better off investing your energy and time into something you're proficient at. This is a dangerous idea that could hinder your progress in learning. If you're unable to overcome challenges and regain your confidence and focus that are essential to acquire new knowledge, you'll rapidly lose enthusiasm and lose motivation to continue forward with your learning.

The Four Steps to Transform an error into a productive Experience

Each person has their own method of handling the failures. Be the one who is willing to accept mistakes and sees them as opportunities to learn rather than as a reason to be discouraged. Making mistakes when learning is actually an chance to utilize the knowledge you gained from them to improve your learning and become more successful in the long process. There are four key actions to follow when adopting this method of thinking for yourself:

1.Acknowledge and accept the error

Accepting that you've made a mistake , and acknowledging that it was the consequence of your mistakes is a must however it is much more difficult to admit than do. If you blame someone else to take the blame for your mistakes, it can be extremely detrimental to yourself. Instead of learning from your experience, you're getting further off the track. The most successful learners and the most prudent are willing to admit their own mistakes, and even willing to admit their mistakes. Even if the error was partially their fault, they want to take responsibility for their actions. They are grateful for these instances and consider them occasions to learn that can provide them with valuable details on how to proceed (or things to avoid) as they continue their journey to learning. Once you accept that you are accountable for your mistakes, even just by telling others about it and acknowledging it on your own behalf--you gain more knowledge to aid you in your journey.

2. Think about what your experience could be will be teaching you.

Take a moment to think about what you are getting out of this incident. Find out the reasons you made a mistake and what you should do to avoid the same mistakes and move forward. Think about the steps you followed to get to the error, and then review it several times over your head. Be aware of how other people did it differently and what they did to move forward. Get advice from your instructor , or any person who can offer direction. Be sure to research the lessons you learned from your mistakes If necessary repeat the mistake until you are able to figure out the issue. Think about it for as many times as you'd like until you feel comfortable enough to proceed.

3. Don't be hesitant when making changes

Making changes to your method can be a challenge, particularly when you've gotten used to your way after working in a particular way for quite a while in the past. If your method of choice was successful the moment, it might be difficult to admit that there are some adjustments to be implemented. This could mean one small change, or a complete overhaul of your plan. In the latter scenario it can be difficult as you could have to overcome more obstacles in your attempt to become proficient on your new methods. It's possible to have to engage in many trials and error, which can be very frustrating. It may not be apparent to you how to correct your error but all you realize is that you have to do something different to get the desired outcome. This requires an enormous amount of energy and perseverance and you must remain focused on your goals. Keep your head down and overcome any doubts regarding your abilities. If necessary, you can laugh at yourself and your situation at times, but keep it fun. The most important thing to remember in the whole thing is to never quit. If you are able to get over these road bumps and overcome any obstacle that comes up further down the road and it'll be impossible to fail.

4. Re-evaluate the situation and reflect on what you learned from the incident.

It is essential to get yourself to be able to appreciate and eagerly anticipating any stumbling blocks you encounter in your learning process. It is important to see them as opportunities to grow in your learning. Once you've remediated an error and discovered the way to get over the issue, you should review the entire experience. Consider how the mistake has caused you to place a particular attention to that particular aspect of learning and how it provided you with an insight from a professional. Consider if your abilities would be the same they are today in the event that you didn't encounter this challenge and then figured out an escape route. Retrospectively examining the significance of your error regardless of how difficult you were, can guarantee that you be able to trust in your abilities and knowledge to overcome any challenges you face later on. The next chapter will teach you how to create an objective for yourself and guide you to steer the ship ahead in full-speed.

Chapter 9: Goal Formulations What to Be Looking For?

Goals aren't the same goal They differ in vague goals as well as specially designed goals. In the next test, you'll be able to see whether you're already experienced when it comes to formulating goals. Note which formulas you believe have been "formulated with concrete language" or "vaguely formulating." Afficiently-formulated goals can be thought of as "vaguely phrased."

Below, I'll provide examples of clear and vague goals and their formulations. For those with overly vague goal formulation you will find a post on the reason the reason why the goal formulation isn't working or suggestions to improve the vague formulation. If the goal formulation is accurate I've also mentioned the correctness in the comment. I'd like to make you familiar with some of the safety hazards for tripping that are commonly missed to "greenhorns."

Example 1. I will not interrupt my work for a half hour for other, more enjoyable pursuits.

Comment: Always set goals with a positive attitude. It is impossible to achieve "nothing," and you can't envision "doing nothing" The brain has there are no negatives.

Example 2: I'd like to hold a leadership position within the company in which I am employed.

Comment: Schedule an appointment. The goal shouldn't become an "endless project." You should set a deadline for when you've reached your goal. Make sure you specify your goal in detail. If you've got an exact scenario in mind the goal will be clear. It is possible to define your objective by asking one of the following:

What kind of leadership position do really want? How many levels of the ladder do I hope to climb?

What department should this leadership role in which department?

How large should my area of responsibility be, so that I still be able to perform effectively?

Do you want to work on my own or with a group?

What could I do to achieve this final goal? What am I willing to give up?

Set a goal for yourself. It is only possible to establish objectives for yourself. Only your actions can lead your goals to be achieved. It is not your decision who is the person who holds a leadership position within the company.

Example 3: I'd like to refresh my understanding of Spanish and following the four-week vacation within Spain in April, I am able to make an effortless conversing in Spanish.

Comment: This is a complete formulation of the goal.

Example 4: I would like the Project Leader to be able, in accordance with our agreement to lead each weekly session in a goal-driven and in a timely manner.

Comment: You only have the ability to establish targets for yourself. Does the project manager follow the things you have told him to do?

Example 5: I would like to be Chancellor.

Comment Make yourself an achievable target. You must be able to reach the goal you have set for yourself. If not, the failure has already been written. Take note of the resources of time and money you've got, the commitments you are making that are in opposition to your goal and the skills you possess. Your goal must be achievable for you. (It is extremely unlikely that someone with excellent election predictions will choose this route;))

Make a plan so you are able to influence the outcome by yourself. Only your attitude can lead you to reach your objective. Even If you were the top person for this chapter, it is the voters who will determine who would win the election.

6. In the near future my supervisor will no ever critique me in front my colleagues.

Comment: You only create targets for yourself. Your boss will not alter his behavior if you wish to. Create your goal in a positive way. It is impossible to

101

accomplish "nothing," and you are not imagining "doing nothing" because our brains can sense nothing negative. In this scenario, you'll need to think about how you could enhance the conversational culture.

Example 7: In an entire year, I'd like to get another job with the company that has more management responsibility and is more lucrative than the one I am currently working at.

Comments: in this instance the aim isn't "only" contingent on you conduct. Because you only have the power to alter your behavior, you'd need to design the goals in such that the external environment don't determine the outcome. You don't decide who gets hired for what job. However, you can consider, for instance, how much you'd like to make yourself look like a professional.

8. Example: I would like to be healthier.

Comment: Schedule an appointment. Your goal should not have the appearance of your only goal. It should not be considered an "endless undertaking." You should set a deadline by which you're hoping to get to your goal. Be specific about your goals. When you have a specific scenario in your mind, is your goal crystal clear.

Create your goal in a way that is observable. What do you know when you are better than you did the past? What would an impartial observer be able to discern - are you doing more exercise? Have you made any changes to your diet?

Example 9: I'd like to finish all lessons in this course within two weeks.

Comment: This is a complete formulation of the goal.

Chapter 10: The Accelerated Learning Techniques

If you decide to try the speed of learning method, you'll discover that there are a variety of things that you can try to improve you learning experiences, aid you to learn faster and enable you to be able to learn anything.

Some people affirm that you learn faster and with more efficiency by teaching or tutoring an individual in something you're also learning. This provides you with a greater motivation to learn and better explain it and you'd be able to explain the same thing to yourself too. You can try the system which we covered during the last chapter by doing short intervals. Between 30 and 45 minutes is enough, with 20 to 30 minute brakes. This will allow you to study for the longest time, without feeling tired or irritable. If you are the one responsible for the success of someone else and success, you can explain the process more clearly and be able to comprehend a large portion of the subject you are teaching in addition.

Talking to yourself in a quiet voice is another thing can be helpful. This can help you to understand the concept a bit more. In addition, it can help you practise reading aloud.

This is also connected to another method can be used: using different senses. While reading (using your senses of vision clearly) it could become monotonous and feel like you're always doing the same routine. It is possible to read with your mouth, but you can create models and draw them. There are a variety of things you can do to boost your education experience!

Writing using your own language is something you can benefit from. Learning from what someone else has taught you and turning it into words you are able to comprehend is among the most beneficial ways to go when looking for a way to determine the best way to understand something. If you are given the chance to revise something or alter the way you read it to comprehend it better, take advantage of it. You may benefit from it more than you realize.

Utilize the 80/20 principle. If you're practicing accelerated learning, you're encouraged to apply the 80/20 principle which says that 80percent of your success is due to 20% of the work you do. The idea is to avoid wasting your time on the remaining 20% of your work, since it's not really necessary! This can save you lots of time, and will help you to manage your time much more efficiently than before.

Another crucial skill you need to master is the art of shutting out distractions. For example, putting away your phone, putting the iPad in the bedroom, and removing everything you do not need on your computer are just a few options to make your study experience more productive.

You might also find it easier to study in other locations, if you are finding you prefer sitting in a calm space with the sound of the air conditioner or heater can help you concentrate more so you choose to do it. If you feel that a noisy place can help you get more done and accomplish everything you have to accomplish and completed, then go to a noisy cafe! It's all about your individual preferences.

It is essential to practice when trying to master new skills There's a reason it's part of the speedy learning process! When you are practicing something, you are exercising the brain's area known as the cerebellum. It is the brain part which is responsible for every movement and action that are innate to you as time passes.

As an example as in your early years and learning to write and draw, you had to concentrate on the fingers you needed to stretch to grip the pen in an effective grip. It's now a natural process when you take out the pencil or pen and begin writing.

This is the case when you're learning the new skill. After you've practiced it for a long time, it is absorbed into your brain and becomes almost irresistible; just as if you were riding a bike according to some.

The thing is that as you begin to master the technique and it becomes natural it is important to continue practicing it. It's similar to exercising. If exercising, the body starts to feel great and you'll be able to perform more and run faster, however when you stop running some time, your cardiovascular drops. It isn't the same amount of time as you used to. This is because of the reality that you've been unable to keep up with your training. In order to get back to running, you must either begin at the beginning from scratch or to practice once more before you lose your ability completely. Be aware that in the first paragraph, I wrote "almost memorable."

Chapter 11: Avoiding the Negative

In the past, we've discussed what self-discipline means and where it originates and also how managing time is among - or perhaps the most important of the essential elements of the character characteristic. In this section, we'll stray slightly by not talking about what you can do to become a better disciplined person, but certain things that you shouldn't do.

It's not just about forming good habits like time management, but it's equally about removing bad habits. This book will speak about the subject in general terms, since every person's personal objectives and habits are different. However, regardless of the numerous individual aspects that could erode the self-control of a person there are some big things that people believe to be the most significant causes of failure for those who wish to improve their self-control.

The most important of these is the much-dreaded excessive. Depeche Mode once said, "Everything is important in huge amounts." So, let me to say that perhaps Martin Gore had a little some issues with excess and consequently could have benefited from some self-control.

I'm not intending to criticize Depeche Mode, because the fact is that excess is something that a lot of people are unable to quit, especially in America that many believe is "the country of abundance." In regards to their favorite things eating, or watching or doing, lots of people aren't simply lacking self-control, they also lack complete control!

I'm aware that prior to the time I was able to control myself my biggest enemy was the large portion of Ben & Jerry's ice cream I could eat in one bite. It's likely that you've had the same moment, when that first taste or your first encounter with something is amazing that, of course, you'll go back for another. However, this can be an incline and, before you realize it, you're in a state of autopilot. A part of me believes that when we make this choice for ourselves, it's probably not actually enjoying the food that we're consuming too much of We just think that we're enjoying it because the first bite was delicious and we'd like to relive that taste and again. Instead of quitting the ice cream or switching off the game - or, in chapter 2 and removing ourselves from social media, we keep eating. This is a shame as if one could just stop doing the thing they've been enjoying too much of, they'll be able to revisit it another day and stand the chance to experience the first sensation of bliss once more. The time away makes the heart feel more affectionate it seems.

It's, of course another issue that occurs when we're inactive about self-control rather than actively. It's easy to indulge that isn't being attentive or totally involved in the particular thing (eating or drinking, or watching television) even though there's a little voice at the back of our heads telling us that we need to stop.

In addition to making a schedule and adhering the plan, I think that avoiding excessive behavior is the most challenging element of developing disciplined self-control. But, as with managing time when you establish certain positive habits (in this instance it's about eliminating those that aren't good) things will begin to become more simple.

The next page will provide some tips that can help you tell yourself "no" to excessive indulgence.

1. Set a limit

The most simple solution is often the easiest one, and this is certainly the case in this instance. To prevent yourself from drinking excessive amounts of something similar to an entire pint of and Jerry's, it is necessary to be conscious of what you'll be able to consume, or, more specifically the amount you'll allow yourself to consume. Imagine this as a commitment to yourself. If you don't keep your word by exceeding the limit that you have set it will be lying to yourself which is not what anyone wants.

It doesn't matter what such as food, TV, or drinks, or food; all you need to do is to set a certain amount of space and when the limit is reached and you're done, you're done. It's over. It doesn't matter if not full, nor this episode ended with the most bizarre cliff-hanger of ever. To be able to have a good, well-developed self-control, you must have the capacity to manage what you're doing to yourself. This is having the courage to convince yourself that you've had enough.

If you require further assistance on this, you may include certain activities to your calendar following Chapter 2. For example, if you often play video games or just watch TV for too long, you could reserve a certain amount of time to complete these things to ensure that you don't indulge in too much.

2. Do not fall prey to the temptation

For certain people, it's not enough to simply establish a limit. Anyone who's experienced a recovery from addiction is aware that in order to avoid relapse into the substance they were dependent on, they must to stay away from getting close to the particular substance for a second time if they want to keep their sobriety. Naturally that having an addiction to sweets or spending too much time on TV isn't as serious as being dependent on an addictive substance However, for those who can't resist it is possible that the same principles could be used.

If you're one of those who can't resist temptation, it's important to realize that it's not a sign that you're in weakness to stay away from things that you are prone to indulge in within your range. Actually making the necessary changes to get rid of those habits out of your daily routine is an indication of self-control! Recognizing that you're not in control in a specific subject and taking the steps to make up for it can help you develop excellent habitual behaviors over time.

For instance I knew a person at high school who got into the video game World of Warcraft, when it was at the height of its popularity while I'm not an expert in addiction I can state with some certainty that he was actually addicted to the game. After returning from school the next day, he'd rush to finish his work before logging on to the internet. He would sleep through the night playing games, then get some sleeping in, and then get up at dawn to squeeze a few hours in before heading to school. The game eventually reached the point where we seldom were seen together in the absence of class. Fortunately for him, when the situation became so bad the student was beginning to ignore his academic obligations, his parents removed his computer. After a month of to a cold diet, he admitted to me that he was shocked by how much time he spent playing the game. When he finally got his computer back, he removed it from the system.

In contrast to my friend, the majority of adults aren't able to have parents to forcefully curb their excessive consumption. Instead, it's the responsibility of them to know that they're drinking too much of something and it's up for them to take action to stop it, even if it means cutting off the item completely.

3. Don't let yourself be deprived of life's small pleasures

Like most items in our lives, there isn't anything that can be described as black or white. Most of the time it's the grey zone and this is certainly for both bad and good practices. I certainly don't want to convince you that good self-control requires you to give up every thing you like for example, sweet foods or a good television show. I enjoy these things as much as any other person and enjoying these things makes our lives more enjoyable.

What I'm saying is that focusing on moderateness and staying clear of excess are the keys to being more content as it lets you take pleasure in a small portion of everything in life instead of many just one or two things. If you do this, you're likely to experience a greater satisfaction from experiencing these particular things, while in the same time, staying clear of excessive amounts of each one.

At the end of the day, however it's all about being in balance. Self-control doesn't mean that you don't treat yourself any more; it's the fact that you've been able to stop going through the motions and are more aware of the type of life you'd like to live for yourself. If you've planned to go out for a few minutes each weekly to work out, you could certainly indulge in some frozen treats after an extended day. If you're working in your passion like a blog, painting, a book, or something else you can lounge in the sofa and watch a show the TV show that you're obsessed with. There's not any single way to determine the amount you should consume because everyone is unique. It's your responsibility to determine what constitutes an appropriate amount of something and it is your responsibility to keep reviewing your lifestyle and habits.

Chapter 12 How Can Speed Reading Focus on Your Objectives?

Reading the Art of Reading

Human beings appear to have an inherent desire of never stopping to improve the quality of life. The invention of the wheel led to massive changes to the world from the grinding of flour to transport. What would we be doing today if not for the simple invention of the wheel? However, it required the human mind to move this breakthrough to the next level.

In the current world it's sometimes as if the saying of every man for himself is true. It's not a secret that we're obliged to put in the effort in order to lead a full and fulfilling life. But knowledge isn't enough. Additionally you need faith to push this knowledge forward.

* Speed reading gives you the information you need.

Self-improvement gives you confidence.

By self-improvement, you'll be more aware about your "sense that you are a person." Then, you begin to discover new opportunities , so that your "self" will develop. Humans can achieve such amazing feats.

If you improve your living conditions, you'll be able to be able to access doors that were closed. There's a wealth of knowledge passed down from generation to generation. Keep the passion that drives us and let it take you to places you've not yet reached.

While you will never be able to know all there is, you can start to comprehend a little. One way to get there is to study the information expressed in words. There is so much reading material in our society that a lifetime of reading isn't enough to cover the entire collection. This is why the art of speed reading can be your method of tapping into the wealth of information available. Speed read.

Learn and Speed Read

If you read to learn there are many who advise reading words slowly, with a rate of about 100-200 words per minute (wpm). This pace is much more slow than the reading speed of a book, that averages between 200 and 400 wpm. However, when you read speed you can read 700 wpm. And, if you follow the right method you'll as well be developing.

The secret to speed reading lies not in how fast you can read texts, it's rather the quality of the words you are reading. When you read speed you'll learn to pick out the essential words and skip the irrelevant words. You'll be able to gain the ability to read the vast amount of text in record time, since it's not required to read every word of the text.

Body Movements while Reading

To master speed reading it is important to identify a few mistakes you'll have to address at the start. These are likely habits that you weren't aware you had

Talking to Youself

As with most of us there is a chance that at some point during your reading session, you'll use the words while you are reading them. It could happen within your mind, or in public. It could be something you decide to do while you're doing your homework. Thinking that you will recall more information if you speak them out loud or inside your mind. The issue with this way for reading is you'll be slow to read as you rush through each word. Your brain is trying to stimulate neural pathways to perform this job. Physical activities that you perform, like muscle movement as well as listening, and even using your voice, are making use of more energy which is going to waste. The actions you take can slow you down and you'll only be able to master a few things by using this method. Don't repeat phrases in your head or out loud. Of course, it is important to be able to record the words you hear in your head However, you don't have to be focusing on one word for too long.

Re-reading

How many times have you have to read the same sentence again due to distraction from the background? Perhaps you don't even know the meaning of the phrase? It's like an obsessional disorder (OCD) because you keep reading the same text repeatedly. This habit will lead you to nowhere quickly. When you are able to accelerate your reading, the need should go away.

Eye Motions

There is a chance to create a complete book about this subject alone since it's so broad. It's obvious that eyes are the primary instrument to focus on words, however they are much more than the above. Eyes don't just move along a line across the page, they also make fast movements that are interrupted by stops. The less they read the less eyes have to perform, and you'll avoid getting that exhausted eye syndrome. Eye movement plays an important part for speedy reading. It is not just a matter of learning to decrease eye movements but also cut out peripheral vision to ensure that you aren't distracted in any way.

Vocabulary

It is said that the greater the amount of books you've read, more your vocabulary gets. When you read speed, that is even more this is the situation.

It's an egg and chicken scenario. Learn more vocabulary and having a wider vocabulary can help speed up the pace of reading. Speed reading means that you are able to read more, and the cycle continues. As many words as you can store in your mind and the more quickly you take in information. You'll notice yourself pause less often when you are faced with unfamiliar words because of the greater vocabulary you have.

In all likelihood, reading is an essential capability for mastering new topics. When you gain more understanding, it will result in new abilities and enhance your life opportunities. Wouldn't it seem like logical that speed reading could make the chances of getting a job? If you're able to read fast you're more likely to read texts beyond your normal reading materials and in your comfort zone. Once you reach this point, you're well on the way to bettering your career prospects. You'll become an engaged person.

Skim Reading

A lot of us employ skim read whenever we need to look up something that's not particularly engaging. Both speed and skim reading make use of quick eye movements. The brain, however, responds differently to different techniques of reading.

If you read a book skimmed you're only getting an outline of text and aren't absorbing any particular information. The brain doesn't get strained in any way since when you come across an unfamiliar word you are free to avoid it. This is the same for complex sentences. You're not learning anything since you're not processing large amounts of information.

When you speed read, or scanning, you're still learning. When you master the skills they will help you to extract information and statistics. You'll be taking in details and will be learning new terms.

Stop skimming reading and learn do a scan (speed read) instead.

Chapter 13: What to Learn Anything in a Month Or More

The last step in rapid learning is to put the various strategies you are planning to implement to create a unified learning system. The system you choose to use should be designed to your individual reactions to environmental conditions and also the method you prefer to learn new material. You should already have played around with various methods of learning and environments to determine which one is most suitable for you. Once you have figured out what is working best, you'll be able to design an instructional system which will guarantee that you will get the most outcomes in the time and effort you devote to learning about any topic. Take the time to note down the best methods and learning environments to be certain that you are putting your knowledge to good use. By using this method of learning, you'll be able to take on any subject, big even small and achieve significant progress in one months or less.

Once you've made a list of useful learning strategies and learning environments, you'll have pick a topic to focus on. It can be a broad topic or small, since the method of learning is generally the same in both cases. If you select a topic that is large like learning a new language, you must realize that while a month of study will provide you with an excellent foundation in the language, but will not let you be fluent within that time. But, one month will suffice to make you a conversational speaker with any other language which is the main goal people seek when learning the language of their choice. If you decide to keep in the process of learning a language, the same strategies will yield rapid results every step.

If you've decided to choose a more extensive area to research, the next step is to break it down into smaller and manageable segments. This allows you to spread out the task into four equal parts throughout one month, and also helping you keep track of your progress over this period of time. After you've divided the content into four parts, you can begin to put in place your own custom learning system!

Week 1

* You've already broken down your topic into four small pieces that correspond to each week. Start with the first one and break it into seven or five smaller pieces-- one for each day you intend to spend studying. You don't have to do it for seven consecutive days, but you can break it down into smaller chunks by studying for two days and then taking a break after which you can study for three days before taking a second day off. Avoid taking two days off at the same time since this makes it more difficult to return to the routine of your studies.

Select the location and time of the day that you'd like to learn. Make sure you set aside the same amount of time per session, and ensure that it's during the same period. A routine can be extremely useful during this process.

* Be sure to have all the resources you require. You must have multiple types of formats to study that include auditory, visual and tactile, or hands-on. Certain topics may require auditory and visual only therefore, you should use at least these two methods.

* If you would like to study alongside others, make a plan with them. You might want to switch between studying by yourself and studying with others, based on what is best for you.

• Finally, schedule the time to check the new knowledge you have acquired. This test should be in the form of actual tests as well as demonstrating the subject to other people. After you've tested yourself and feel confident about your knowledge of the subject, then you are able organize a class where you can teach the subject to other people. If teaching the subject to others isn't feasible and you are not confident, just put the information to use. If it is an unfamiliar language, try practicing what you've learned by working in a conversation with native speakers. If it's something more concrete such as cooking or building work do what you've learned in a real-world situation. Resolve what you learned to fix, bake what it was you learned to bake and the list goes on. This is a crucial procedure that should be completed at the conclusion of each week before going on to the next one.

Repeat this procedure to weeks 2, and 4, focusing on one daily segment per day as well as one weekly segment every week. If there is a problem that occurs and you are forced to miss one day, simply continue the best way you can. Be sure to complete additional work every day until you are caught up. The one thing you do not would like to do is be in a rut over a long period of time. A well-organized system demands the use of a well-planned plan.

It's safe to say that the first time you try this method into practice will likely not be the easiest of occasions. There will be things you didn't expect and challenges you did not expect to come across. Don't get discouraged by this. Your first attempt at this will be an educational experience that will be a learning experience on multiple levels. You'll be able to perfect your system of accelerated learning as you use it. In the end, it will function smoothly and effortlessly, allowing the user to deal with any subject in any amount without fear and confidence.

Chapter 14: A Few Other Techniques

In the present, there are too many distractions that can divert our attention from our work. However, if you'd like to learn to retain information more quickly and be a better student, there are some strategies that can aid you in doubling or even more than triple how much information that you keep in your time. If you allow yourself to be distracted , you make it more difficult it is for your mind to simply absorb the information you're presenting. When you have other distractions, such as joking about the place of your the mind's attention, it makes you be even more focused to remember what you have read.

If you're an avid music fan, try to listen to music that does not have the lyrics. Music that has lyrics could hinder your ability to process language. If you are listening to music that has lots of lyrics, you're basically destroying your own abilities. Your brain will not be able to focus completely on one piece of information as the others can be either written or spoken and will disrupt your flow. Instead, try listening at music which is solely instrumental. If you are able to stay away from music that contains lyrics, you can still listen to music that are playing in the background. This will not distract yourself from the content and making learning and retention simpler.

Make sure you choose the time slots that are conducive for studying. If you work in a time when you are likely to get interrupted you'll easily get distracted by each interruption, making it more difficult for you. Be sure to plan for times when you are energized. If you're exhausted, your mind will be in a state of clarity and ready to perform the kinds of mental gymnastics that you want to do. You wouldn't ask your body to run a marathon if you're tired, therefore why would you ask the same thing of your brain? It's a muscle as well. By keeping the distractions to a minimum, and feeling well-rested, you're also less likely to be stressed when studying, which could ease your burden.

The more stressed you are, the more difficult it is to focus on the task you are working on.

With the modern technology that is available, it is extremely difficult to be disconnected from the world in the world. With a cell phone that is always on, you're connected to anyone at any time. The constant connectivity can be very distracting. engaging with your friends, or finding out what someone else has posted on Facebook is a lot more entertaining than the work you're trying to do. If you wish to learn and remember the data that you're working with, it is essential to make a conscious effort to remove yourself from the world that surrounds you. Disable notifications, cell phones or whatever else you have to do to stay focused on your task at present. This is a difficult task for some people , especially those who haven't done this before. If that's the case , then take a few minutes at an interval. Don't get yourself into a state of disarray by not being connected since that will not accomplish any results.

133

Many students study in a sitting position or lying down. Although this state of relaxation can aid in keeping your attention on one specific thing and one thing only, you should not remain in a slumber for the duration of your study. Moving around and standing during breaks can increase blood flow and also energy in your body. Both of these are beneficial for keeping you energized and fresh. Also, you'll give an increase in oxygen supply to your brain due to an increased flow of blood. And the more oxygen you provide to your brain, the better it functions.

Make a list of the content you're about to read. If you are feeling confident in certain aspects of the information you covering, then you must skip these parts and look over the ones you're less confident about. When you look over information that you already have a good understanding with, you could create the illusion of security. It will make you feel as if you are more knowledgeable and spend your time from the facts that need your focus. It also increases the amount of information you're not aware of, helping you achieve the highest level of retention of all the subjects that you're trying to remember.

Write yourself a story. This one isn't enough to be stressed If you can come up with an engaging story to reveal the information you're trying to master, it's great and should be read. However, if you're able to create an original story, by putting facts into a story that is relatable, the brain is going to have a better time remembering it, rather than trying to process tiny pieces of information. Sharing your story with another person or even trying to instruct them on the subject will help you retain it better. If you are teaching someone else, you have to modify the content and then put it into bite-sized chunks that are easy to someone who isn't familiar with the subject. Rewriting the material and forcing yourself to work hard with the concepts will provide you with greater understanding and make it easier to comprehend.

Another suggestion to remember is to look up and try to preview the material you're going to cover. By visiting other websites or looking up other books prior to getting down to serious studying or memorization, you'll be able to provide a different an understanding of material that may not be obvious from the book you are currently studying. It will help you understand the material better. it also gives you a an alternative perspective that will help the information stick in your head and aid you to retain the information better. It can also help you get an overall picture when you read a few lines before reading in full. You'll be better in a position to know what direction the text is taking and hopefully, by creating an increase in recognition within your brain, you'll be strengthening certain pathways within your brain.

Chapter 15: Mindfulness-based Activities that improve brainpower and memory

Mindfulness can be a powerful cure to many issues.

Most of us complain about being distracted. We complain that we aren't efficient enough. We complain that we are unable to remember information or remember it at the right time.

We often do not be aware of is that the main reason behind all of these problems is a lack of awareness. A state of complete mindfulness assists us in achieving this.

Being mindful means being conscious of the present and the things that it brings to it without thinking about the past or the future. This allows you to focus on "what's happening now and lets you focus on the present moment in order to be more deeply absorbed and in the moment.

If you think about this, you'll see that this is exactly what is required to remain conscious, alert, and alert to process information effectively and without attaching labels to it. Think critically, encode information in a way that is correct and then consolidate it in the long-term memory, and then retrieve it when we need it.

Let's discuss some incredible methods of mindfulness that can assist you in increasing your capacity to process thoughts, think and remember memories.

Eat mindfully

Mindfulness is a state that you usually experience when you're in a position to be conscious of all you do, how you experience and everything you see. It takes time and perseverance for you to achieve this level, you have to begin by making small effort every day. A mindful diet is a simple method of doing that.

Each when you sit down to an evening meal, do the following suggestions and if you begin to practice these simple actions, you'll be able to complete your chores with greater focus , which will enhance your memory.

Eat in a quiet, distraction free place. Also, turn off the TV to allow you to dine in peace and be completely focused on your food. It can be a challenge however, if you establish the habit of eating in silence and focusing on your food, you'll soon appreciate the value of this experience.

Make a small portion of the food you are planning to eat, so that you concentrate on a tiny piece at a moment instead of eating enough food to fill your stomach. This helps you develop an habit of breaking information into chunks to make it easier to understand it more efficiently.

Make small bites, take each one and chew it thoroughly and slowly before swallowing it down. The more often you do this and the more you do it, the more you begin to notice various textures, tastes, and smells and the more you'll enjoy the sensation. This will allow you to take in the food you have on your plate, pay attention to only one aspect of the information at one time, and engage all your senses into the experience. In time, this routine will improve and strengthen your cognitive abilities as well as the ability to absorb information. Additionally, it will enable you to be present take it in, enjoy itand enjoy it.

Don't label your food as bad or good; make sure you choose the right adjectives based on the flavor and texture, smell, and overall impression. If something tastes sour label it as rather than bad. If something is sweet, refer to it as that instead of labelling it as unpalatable. This will help you see things in the context of what they are, get precise information, and make rational decisions.

Eat your food to keep your attention on the task each time your mind wanders. The mind's wandering is normal and you must be patient when you realize that wandering has taken place. Keep your attention on eating and enjoying your meal so long as you continue doing this, you're trying to remain mindful.

If you eat according to the pattern that I have described above, every time you sit down for food or snacks and you become aware of eating. You will begin eating with a calm and relaxed attitude, taking more pleasure in your food and being grateful of it. In addition, be able to recognize when you require and don't require food to sustain yourself.

Make sure you are mindful in all tasks.

Apply the principles you have learned from mindful eating for all other activities such as chores, routine activities such as walking and reading, playing about research, meeting with clients, presenting presentations etc. This will ensure that each time you perform a task you perform it with total awareness focus your whole heart and mind on the task, put your attention entirely on it and ensure that you encode information efficiently.

This means that you should follow these steps every whenever you're working on something whether it's watching a film or making a written report:

Imagine the task you're planning to accomplish and speak it out loud.

Visualize yourself doing the task and then sketch out the plan in your head.

Start slow and take note of the details so that you can fully immerse yourself into the journey.

The next step should be taken gradually and concentrate on the task at hand.

If your mind wanders When your mind wanders, return it to the task at hand.

When you have completed each task, evaluate your efficiency and recall the steps and reflect on the lessons you have gained from it. Remember all the details you needed to remember and note it down If you can. Doing these exercises consistently will be a boon to your brain power.

Pay attention and observe

Most of us make poor or ineffective decisions as a result of the various things we observe and hear to that cloud our judgement in our capacity to be clear. Our preconceived ideas usually make us to hear and view things through their dirty lenses. This is the reason we struggle in coding information accurately and effectively.

The solution to this problem is to help your brain learn to pay attention to and pay attention to things. When you notice something, don't focus on it according to your preconceived notions. Instead, examine it as it actually is. When you listen to something, do it in a calm, non-judgmental and sincerely. Use this information to your advantage in everything you listen to and observe. In the next few weeks, your capacity to process information quickly will increase, as is your ability to remember it.

Mindfulness-based meditation

Mindfulness-based meditation is an easy, relaxing and beautiful method which teaches you to remain in the present moment be in it, cherish it, and appreciate the moment. It improves your ability to concentrate on a single job and to encode, collect the information, organize it, and store information efficiently.

Here's a simple meditation practice that is based on mindfulness:

Relax and enjoy any posture you want to; ensure you're in a calm space too.

143

Be aware of your breath, and pay attention calmly as you breathe in through your nose and exhale out of your mouth.

Take note of your breathing and pay attention to it when it is introduced into your body, rotates inside, and slowly goes out as an out-breath.

If you notice that you've lost yourself in thoughts Return your focus to your breath and your body and pay attention to them.

Do this for between 2 and 5 minutes, and gradually increase the time spent practicing.

Make sure to do this at least each day, and at each time you need to accomplish a task that is important.

As you become aware of your own work and duties take note of your diet and health too.

Chapter 16: Speed Reading Techniques

If you're analyzing an Shakespearean play in your literature class, or are browsing through an article which you'll have to master in the future it can be boring for certain. Reading speed could be an approach that can aid in learning faster. While it is true that reading faster can lead in lower learning. However, with training, you can counter this issue.

Avoid Subvocalizing

You may have noticed that while reading, you're subvocalizing and moving the mouth while you attempt to communicate the words aloud to yourself. This can aid you in remembering some ideas however it can be a major obstacle to learning faster. A simple way to overcome the habit of chewing on gum while you read. This can stimulate muscles that are employed to subvocalize.

Beware of reading words that you have already read

When you read your eyes will are likely to go back to words from the past. The majority of the time they are a few seconds that do not aid you in enhancing your memory. You can make use of the index cards to help you remember the words after reading them. This can also occur when you fail to comprehend the words you're reading. If your eyes seem to be bouncing multiple lines back that is a sign that you need to slow down.

Pay attention to your eye Moves

While reading your eyes can wander around in a erratic manner, skipping words while pausing for others. Be aware that you can only read effectively if your eyes are stable. If you move your eyes less frequently for each line, you'll be able to read much faster. But be careful. Recent research suggests limitations to what you can be reading at the same time:

The human eye is able to detect only 4 letters on the left of the eye position, but eight alphabets to your right. In the average, that's approximately 2 to 3 words in one go.

There are letters about nine to fifteen spaces right in front of your eyes. However, you won't be able to comprehend them.

Regular readers are unable to comprehend words that are on other lines. Learning to read fast by skipping lines, while still understanding them can be a serious problem.

Train Your Eyes to make fewer movements The brain of the human being can determine which direction to focus our eyes based on how long or familiar next words appear. It is possible to read more quickly if you exercise your eyes to move towards specific areas of the page. Below is an exercise that you could try:

147

Place an index card on top of an unwritten text line.

In the blank card draw an"X" over the first word.

Then make another X. Include three additional words to make it clearer, five words for the basic text and seven words in case you intend just to go through the most important areas.

When you are at the limit of the line, add more X with similar distance.

Take your time reading while you move down on the index, putting in an concentration only to the words just below every one of the X.

You should aim for a speedier pace that you can comprehend

There are programs for speed reading that claim to boost your reading speed by first focusing your reflexes before you practice until your brain can catch up. However, be aware that this method hasn't been confirmed as a valid strategy before. It could help improve the speed at which you go through the information. But, the degree of comprehension may not be sufficient. If you're looking for speedy reading, you could test your skills using the following exercises:

Make use of a pen or pencil to trace the text. Keep track of the time and finish when you get to the end of the line.

Begin by reading for one minute, following the speed that the pencil is moving. Even in the event that you don't understand the words you're reading. Concentrate on the text and keep your eyes moving throughout the entire minute.

Do not stop for more than 30 seconds and then try to increase your speed.

Text Skimming

It is possible to use skimming to get a fundamental knowledge of the subject you are looking to learn. Skimming can help you grasp the fundamental concepts in an instructional book to prepare to take an exam. Note that skimming isn't an ideal option for those who require extensive reading.

Check out the headings and titles

Begin by reading only the chapters' titles and subheadings. This is at the start of main sections.

Find the Start and the End of the section

Textbooks usually include summaries and introductions to each chapter. It is possible to read the beginning and final paragraphs of an article, or chapter. If you're familiar with the subject, you will be able to easily read. But, do not try to read at a high speed. It is possible to reduce time by skipping the majority of the paragraphs. However, it's more important to know the meaning of what you read.

Make sure to highlight important terms throughout the Document

If you're looking to learn quickly, look swiftly across the text instead of reading at a normal speed. After you have read the main points of the article, select the keywords you want to highlight as important areas. Stop and highlight the following words:

Terms are repeated many times

The fundamental concepts usually using terms from the sections headings, titles or the

Proper nouns

The words are in italics in bold letters , or underlined

Words that you aren't sure of what they mean.

Examine Diagrams and Pictures

The diagrams and illustrations generally provide plenty of information with no reading. Make sure you comprehend the purpose of each diagram.

If You're Confused Learn the First Sentence in Every Paragraph

If you've lost the gist of the idea, go through the beginning of each paragraph. Most of the time those first 2 sentences are the best way to remind you on the most important aspects.

Learn the material through your Annotations

Go back to the words you marked. Are you able to comprehend these words and gain a general understanding of what the content is about? If you're confused by the meaning of a particular word, attempt to read a few sentences that surround the word to help remind you of the topic. Make note of any added words when you go through this.

Exercise

Track your progress by keeping track of your reading speed. Do your best to keep up with your speed to remain motivated. Do the following exercise so you can read by WPM or Words Per Minute.

You can count the number of words in a line and multiply that number by the number of lines that are on one page

Set a timer to run for five minutes, and then measure the number of lines you can read within that timeframe.

Multiply the pages you read by the amount pages you've have read. Divide the result by five to calculate your WPM estimate.

There are also online tests to gauge your WPM however, you may have a different reading speed on a printed paper as opposed to a screen.

Your reading speed will improve if you perform these exercises consistently. You may even increase your reading speed in a few weeks. Set your goals to motivate yourself to increase your speed.

200-250 WPM is the ideal range for people 12-year-olds and over.

300 WPM is perfect for college students.

A speed of 450 WPM is recommended for students who are looking for the fundamentals

1000 WPM is considered to be a fast speed that is competitive.

Be aware that understanding the idea will be more crucial than having an unbeatable speed.

Chapter 17: Things Not to Do During Your Interview

We've discussed a variety of things you must do for your interview, and how to prepare. There are a lot of things that you need to try to avoid during the interview process that might not be things you'd think about. A few of these tips might seem obvious, however you'd be shocked at how many candidates make errors that can cost them their job offer.

SAVING UP

Many people fall into the trap of eating too much stress. Stress can manifest in a variety of ways, and one way to do this is to eat empty calories. When you're in a position of pressure to perform, you may make poor decisions and fast that can lead to low body performance.

Your body functions as an instrument and needs the correct type of fuel to function in a efficient manner. Poor food choices are similar to putting the wrong kind of fuel in your vehicle. When you choose the wrong fuel into your car, the engine will not function to its maximum capabilities and it will start to slow down in its functions. Gas mileage will drop and with time the engine may fail completely.

The body of yours is similar in the sense that if you are not providing the correct fuel, your body will begin to begin to break down over time. Most breakdowns aren't evident to anyone else, not even to ourselves. We might not be sleeping enough as we ought to. We may feel exhausted or even experience issues with our moods, but the most harmful and damaging aspect of poor choices with food is the impact on the brain's function.

When we feel stressed, we don't pay any to the kinds of food we put into our bodies. We grab whatever we can available or what our bodies start to want. The most common kind of craving we experience is complex carbohydrates, such as breads or other foods that are of any nutritional worth. Things like sweets and candy are other choices that people could be attracted to.

These sweet foods get into our systems and provide rapid rocket-like burst of energy, but they exhaust fast. They are not nourishing for the body or our brains, or drain the energy sources in the body more quickly than those that are rich in protein. When brain function is impaired, all functions in the autonomic nervous system is slowed down.

The Autonomic nervous system (ANS) is the part of the body that controls the things that happen without thinking. The brain's function, breathing, and digestive function are part in this system. The brain is the primary organ's computer and when the brain's performance slows the body as a whole slows.

Imagine going to an interview after having consumed a lot of stress. You've made some bad decisions and now you are suffering from a severe fog of thought. It is difficult to formulate complete thoughts , and you may stumble over the words. Add to this the anxiety about being with a stranger and being asked questions, and you've got the recipe for catastrophe.

Instead of consuming excessively, try to stay hydrated with plenty of water and eat healthy , nutritious food items. Beware of foods that cause discomfort or are unfamiliar to you. The majority of people are unaware that food allergies could occur within the space of 3 days. Be aware of the foods you eat a few days before your interview since it could have a major impact not just in how your body works but also in making sure that you don't suffer the same reaction. It's not the best time to be innovative in your food choices. Look out for food items that contain a strong odor. Even if you clean your teeth, apply mouthwash, or even chew gum or take a mint to take your breath before your appointment, the strong smell of foods may still come through. What you're left with is the smell of the powerful food and the smell you tried to hide it with. The strong smells can distract the interviewer as well as anyone might meet you during the interview. Your interviewer will be thinking about how you live your life is, and while it's not a major element, it can cause them to wonder if they can handle this smell regular daily basis.

Consume food items that are odorless and do not cause stomach problems. Make sure that the food you eat don't cause stains on your clothing or mouth. A blue sucker before your interview can distract you and the interviewer will only be thinking about why your mouth is blue, instead of paying attentively to the answers they give to their questions that they have thought of.

Do not drink alcohol prior to your interview, or the night prior to. Alcohol can impede your brain's functioning and cognitive capabilities. Your critical thinking could be affected even after the initial effects have faded. Alcohol can also be an antidepressant, so even though you might feel it eases the burden of your anxiety and can make you feel more relaxed, it could let in floods of moods that aren't appropriate for the workplace , and may cause depression. In addition, if your prospective employer is smelling alcohol on you, they'll stay clear of offering you a job because it is an indication of your security when you are employed.

Chapter 18: The Training of Your Brain for Success

The suggestions from the earlier chapter are excellent to get your memory and for a start on the path to be more successful at every aspect of life by giving your brain more efficient to use.

If you want to achieve more than simply remembering some things better You need to develop your brain, rather than just learning some tricks to remember. Here are some strategies to increase your chances of learning at a quicker leveland becoming naturally adept at retaining these bits of information.

Do some work on Memory and creative exercises

It is the only method to keep your brain in top form and start creating a more efficient tool for everyday use is to keep it active. You can try playing memory or puzzle games to stimulate your brain thinking in a variety of ways. It is also worth picking an interest in creativity or something similar to expand your mind.

Your brain is like every other body part and if you don't make use of it regularly, eventually it will go away.

Eat and exercise regularly

The most effective way to take in order to increase the top brain functions is to think of it as to be a total body experience. It is recommended to begin with a new exercise routine and keep it up. It might seem like it isn't related to the development of your brain's strength and strength, but when you exercise and sweat, you release chemicals to your brain, which could help increase your chances of performance. It also helps to clear your mind and help your stress go and improve your concentration abilities.

Apart from working your body, it is important to be thinking about your diet. There's even a set of foods you should try to eat in order to improve your brain and processing abilities. Let's examine what of these food items can provide for you.

Sunflower Seeds

These, as well as other seeds, contain a good mix of vitamin B and omega fatty acids as well as protein. They also contain tryptophan that your brain utilizes to for forming a sense of elevation. It is also possible to eat sprouts of these seeds to get an additional boost.

Tomatoes

Your mood could also be balanced with a diet of tomatoes as they are loaded with Lycopene. This antioxidant will aid in fighting against dementia as well.

Whole Grain Foods

To get more B vitamins carbohydrate, omega fatty acids, and fiber, consider adding whole grain products to your daily diet. These foods will not only improve your cognitive power and improve your overall health, but also to prevent blood clots developing.

Avocado

Avocado is a great source of the healthy fats your brain and body need to function at their optimal rate. They also have potassium, vitamin E and vitamin K. These helps prevent strokes from harming your brain, and keep it running for a long period of duration.

Coconut Oil

To further protect yourself against stroke and dementia You can also include coconut oil in your diet. It can also give your brain more glucose in a healthy manner which is the fuel your brain utilizes to process information faster and make you better at learning.

Beans and Legumes

In order to provide your brain with more nutritious glucose, treat yourself with some legumes and beans. They also contain a healthy dose of vitamin B along with higher levels of omega fatty acids which can be beneficial to your brain.

Blueberries

They are only one of the group of darker berries which can do wonders for the brain's power. They can aid in identifying the signs of dementia, increase the memory of your brain, improve your ability to learn as well as other cognitive capabilities.

Rosemary

Rosemary is a different essential food to keep your brain as sharp as you would like to have it. It aids in your memory as well as your thinking processes, and it's not just because of just the scent. Additionally, it's an uplifting scent and can add to your energy levels It's good for all of us!

Spinach

As a further dementia-fighter, you can incorporate spinach into your diet. It also has folate, vitamin E and folate, which are great for fighting against the threat of stroke, and also making your brain more strong.

Broccoli

Broccoli can be a great source of increasing the brain's power. It's loaded with vitamin K and iron, fiber vitamins B and C as well as calcium, and beta carotene, which helps keep your mind healthy and help you stay at high levels of game.

Chia Seeds

Add these seeds into your diet to gain a healthy quantity of antioxidants. They are also a great source of healthy glucose that boosts brain's power. They are also useful in adding omega fats.

Dark Chocolate

Although you might not instantly decide to make chocolate an appropriate food to begin eating, if you consume the right kinds in the right quantities, you'll be doing a lot for your brain. Dark chocolate isn't just an energy booster however, it is an antioxidant that makes your brain work highest level.

Nuts

One of the best sources for fats that are healthy and essential vitamins your brain requires are walnuts and almonds. Others members in this group are beneficial for you too, however, these two options are the very top to ensure a healthier, more efficient mind.

Quinoa

You might want to consider adding quinoa into your diet too to get more healthy glucose your brain needs. Also, it can be an excellent source of B vitamins that boost your energy levels and mood. These are vital to keep you and active for a long time.

Red Cabbage

Red cabbage is a must to increase the antioxidant levels and improve your brain's performance. It's easy to obtain and cook therefore, you should consider making it a regular part of your meals.

You can do Some Different Things

Apart from finding innovative ways to exercise and improving your fitness and diet Begin to find new things to do with your spare time. Offering your mind a variety of activities that stimulate your interest could help make you more capable of learning more quickly and retain information better. This is the same thinking process as exercising to strengthen your mind to get stronger, you should work it out!

Stop Multitasking

If you're looking to be able to grasp the subject matter in a rapid manner and utilize the brain's greatest potential, then you'll need to be able to focus. Today, people lead very hectic lives and it may seem as if there are things that require your attention all the time , and in many different directions. But, you must get used to not trying to complete more than just one thing at time to eliminate all of those stressors and distractions. It's natural to multi-task and get things completed more efficiently however, it can actually work against you!

Take a break

If you're trying to understand anything new or something you've never done before, you will often feel overwhelmed or caught up with a plethora of information. If you be overwhelmed, you should take a step back. Do not continue to look at it until it ceases to make sense. You can then revisit the subject in a new way and appreciate it better when you step away from it for a while.

Try meditation

It's the right time to start taking steps toward making your brain's power an important aspect of your daily life. The ability to focus your body, mind as well as your spiritual aspect is essential to becoming a better teacher. Discover a few simple meditation methods and make them part of your routine. This will assist you in learning how to focus more effectively, eliminate distractions and focus on one thing at an time. Additionally, it's an excellent habit to begin to improve your overall health!

My opinion is that children, young people as well as college students and even adults can greatly enhance their capacity to learn more quickly when they eat a balanced and balanced diet. Consuming the right food is similar to putting the right gasoline in your car. If there isn't the correct gasoline for a car the vehicle will not operate correctly, and it will run at a lower rate. Similar is the case with your body. Give your body the right nutrition and give it the minerals, vitamins and the daily nutrition it requires and you will see better results.

Begin to incorporate these food choices into your daily diet to help you take your studies to the next step! It's probably one of the most effective actions you can take today to make a significant change!

Chapter 19: Resilience

Watch an infant trying to make his first steps or trying to find the right words to communicate with his. Imagine each successful person who has made a significant contribution to the human race and the way they all resolved not to give up until they have achieved their goals even after failing repeatedly and repeatedly. Imagine a gymnast making the effort to break his personal bests with determination and perseverance. One thing that is common to everyone they share is their strength, and their ability to bounce back.

Resilience is an important ability to evolve. There is a greater chance to live a longer life and be successful when you are able to withstand difficult circumstances. Many times, the home or academic settings, as well as work haven't been helpful in any way to this aspect.

It is a challenge to open up about our struggles once things begin to slide downward. We aren't willing to let others see the work we put into it and the efforts we put into. We cover ourselves because letting people know where we've failed creates a sense of vulnerability and insecurity particularly if it's been inflicted on us during the course of our lives.

Additionally, with a history of both informal and formal learning, such as at school as well as in the home and at home, we are taught to let go when things get tough. Instead of reprimanding children each time they is agitated without reason, whether at home or at public locations such as the mall, parents let the behavior remain. This is a common occurrence. Anybody who is working out to shed weight or trying playing an instrument in the beginning cannot get what he wants If he's not persistent.

Resilience is not taught within inside the confines of the schoolroom, nor is it discussed in the workplace because the emphasis is too heavily on education, but not addressing other fundamental subjects such as resilience. We hinder our ability to progress in our development if we aren't taking an opinion on the subject we're pursuing. Take a look at a child allowed to walk on their own, to one dependent on the "baby walker." The latter, through the natural instincts of his being, progresses through crawling and walking reaching out to the hands of his parents and grasping at the objects that is in his way until, eventually the child is able to walk independently. He develops resilience without having the knowledge. But, the latter is prone to becoming dependent upon his "crutches" and consequently fail to be able to walk independently. A lot of companies have a reward system that fails to inspire resilience, because it encourages the idea of a short-lived reflective mindset which does not help employees understand the importance of taking the time to think things through.

Methods to build resilience can be described as:

Stay up to date with the latest techniques to learn until they are easier.

Take note of every emotion that arises from various aspects of learning, both the good and bad, triggered by various learning experiences.

Make sure you choose challenging learning options.

Test out new learning techniques.

Give a concrete reason why you chose to learn the things you've learned over the years.

Take the time to soak up the excitement and emotion that are a part of the process of learning.

You should ask yourself "What could I do to become better in my learning?"

Recognizing the lessons acquired by chance, or experiences discovered by accident, then add these experiences to your understanding.

Engage in activities that test you to work on your weaknesses , and improve your ability to learn.

Let's look at four areas of resilience, including determination, perseverance, the ability to discover new things, managing the complexities of life, and facing the uncertainty

Tenacity

After having seen how the brain functions better when given time to rest regularly You must learn to deal with pressure, grabbing every opportunity to learn. To make improvements in any area (including the process of learning) it is essential to be able to master the art of persistence, never abandoning your goal until you are extremely proficient in whatever it is you're learning.

In each case there are things that one can try to increase your endurance. This list provides fantastic suggestions for how you can get there.

Make a plan and create tangible objectives in that direction. Keep working until you achieve your goal Do not stop until you find something that you had not imagined at all. If this happens, re-evaluate your goals and then start over.

Always leave a note to your family and friends to inform them that you will not want to disturb them during the duration of your studies. Disable your cell phones and or other devices that could distract you.

Find a quiet spot to keep away from distracting sounds.

If you find yourself having your head floating in the cloud then get up and move around for a few minutes.

Have a light snack to snack on if you are getting hungry. Then, drink water.

Write down the routine activities you typically enjoy, like making a cup of coffee, listening to radio music, and other naiveties which could take up studying time. You can cut it in half!

Invite your friends and colleagues to encourage you to keep studying when you're bored and all you would like to do is get involved in something different.

Learn at different speeds and in different ways. Understanding how you learn best and staying focused on it can make it easier to keep going.

Do a mental inventory of something you've struggled with. Then apply one of the ideas above.

Begin to Explore New Things

As children, all of us begins as adventurers, attempting to discover the world as our minds of the earliest years let us. However, as we age, we lose this enthralling characteristic until it disappears completely.

Already, you've seen how your brain continually searches for information and make sense of it. It is also evident that it likes to put random pieces of information together to create the whole. The most successful learners use the unique patterning method of their minds, yet simultaneously they don't stay at the same time. They continue to seek new methods, researching and asking questions with the intention of expanding the knowledge they already have. They don't mind setting an entirely new way of practice, they are willing to take advantage of every opportunity and are willing to take sensible risks.

If you start to say things like "I cannot follow this pattern in doing that," then you

175

may need to determine whether you're starting to set your routine.

To bring back the sense of adventure, try to do something completely other than what you normally do, even though it could be difficult.

This easy exercise can aid you in getting back to the right mindset. Take a seat and recline. Find the most comfortable position possible. Then, cross your legs and remove them. Repeat the crossing. Did you notice that crossing the exact same area area over twice? If you crossed that same step, then why?

Try crossing your legs in the other way. Take a step forward.

Now do the same thing, crossing your legs in the opposite direction. Now, stand up. Attach your arms to your chest. Then let them fall to your sides. Repeat the procedure. Did you cross the same arm to the other twice? Then cross them the opposite way. Which one is easier?

The majority of people naturally move their dominant leg over the other but are able to turn it around. This is different for arms, though many people find it more difficult crossing their opposite arms, but that's does not mean they cannot quickly master this. It's easy to imagine your brain's interpretation of the new cross-laterality sense while working on this. When you connect both arms you'll discover that this unnatural method can be a precise illustration of what's involved when you attempt to return to the adventurous side of you.

These are some more practical suggestions:

Request your spouse or friend to accompany you on a trip. Set a date and date and time. Let the person pick the location without knowing and then let it take it as it comes.

Take a different route to work. an alternative route or method of transportation.

Take in a concert of the music group you aren't used to.

Visit an organization whose business is quite different from yours and you can learn about them.

How adventurous do you feel? Try some of the suggestions below if you are having trouble to rekindle your passion for adventure. Create a personal list of your own ideas to test them. The people who are able to learn in the current age of technology are like the merchant adventurers of older times or space explorers of Star Trek.

Being able go places other people haven't been requires courage , even if it's just in your mind. Nobel Prize winner and Holocaust survivor Elie Wiesel [9] explained it this way"Life will be meaningless without risk, and everything else, including the risk will be less important if your center is strong.

To be successful, you need to build the foundation of your being. The essence of your being has many faces, and I would like you to know from this book. The core of you is the ability to learn. If you're a skilled learner, then no task will be too challenging for you. You can test the very core of who you are when faced with the challenge of a complex task.

Solving Complex Problems

Many people give up on their path to learning despite having the best intentions, due to a difficult turn and aren't sure what to do about the situation. This is the case when you're competing for an MBA or putting together an entirely new item of furniture or even coaching the local team of football. Whatever you're learning there will be times that you'll get stuck. The anger and frustration will creep into your life, and you may even feel depressed. It is precisely in these situations that you'll need an effective method to deal with the stress.

Here are ten tips you need to be aware of when it becomes difficult to keep your knowledge up to date:

1. Stop doing what you're doing and take an unplanned break.

2. Try to recall what you did last time you were stuck in this manner.

3. Create a chart that outlines your choices.

4. Confide in a person. You can ask them to describe what they'd do if they were in your position.

5 Ask for assistance by reading books.

6 Get answers from the internet.

7 Take part in an exercise, and see what comes up that could be an avenue to get out.

8 Take a break and lie down to tell you that solution is going to find you in the near future.

9 Make a change in your the environment.

10. Ask yourself the most questions you can think of and then provide answers to each of them. It might be a way to assist you in figuring the way out.

Dealing with uncertainty and confusion

We aren't living in a world that could simply move From A to B. Instead it is a journey between F and H using Y. It's as simple and complex as it could sound. The guidelines of life are always changing and an approach to marketing seems to be in line with the norm the day before, the following day, it's not.

Conclusion

I'd like to express my gratitude and congratulate you on completing my lines from beginning to the end.

I hope this book is useful in helping you to learn about the various methods you can employ to increase your memory.

A sharp memory can benefit all aspects that you live, such as your relationships with others and health, financial as well as your career. It's not just a way to impress your friends and family and colleagues, but also maintain your mind in good condition.

Additionally, it can help you avoid being embarrassment at social gatherings when you meet people you know by name but you haven't remembered their name. Being able to recall your name can be lifesaving as it will prevent you from making similar mistakes.

This book is focused on increasing the speed of memory to improve your learning speed and be more efficient. It also explains the ways that certain aspects such as inadequate nutrition can directly impact the brain.

It's also about educating the brain to build an extended working memory. It will help you learn to keep lists, series of names, numbers, as well as a deck of playing cards. It is also training you to be a master of memory and also to keep your brain in good shape even into older age.

I hope you will take the advice and tips that are within this guide. It is not every person who has a sharp memory. You're fortunate to have this book, and you will have the an opportunity to increase your memory.

www.ingramcontent.com/pod-product-compliance
Lightning Source LLC
Chambersburg PA
CBHW060333030426
42336CB00011B/1314